# TOM THE DANCIN

## INTO the TRUMPVERSE

BOOK DESIGN BY ROBBIE ROBBINS

This is the 7th volume in
*The Complete Tom the Dancing Bug.*

TOM THE DANCING BUG: INTO THE TRUMPVERSE
© 2020 RUBEN BOLLING, ALL RIGHTS RESERVED.

FOREWORD © 2020 NEIL GAIMAN

ISBN: 978-1-951038-08-3

FIRST PRINTING AUGUST 2020

4  3  2  1    20  21  22  24

PRINTED IN KOREA

CLOVER PRESS:
ROBBIE ROBBINS, PRESIDENT/ART DIRECTOR
TED ADAMS, PUBLISHER
ELAINE LAROSA, OPERATIONS
NATE MURRAY, BUSINESS DEVELOPMENT
TIM BELL, SHIPPING ASSISTANT
ELIZABETH NEE, MARKETING ASSISTANT

CLOVER ✿ PRESS
SAN DIEGO, CA

# TOM THE DANCING BUG:
# INTO the TRUMPVERSE

Comics
by
**Ruben
Bolling**

# About Tom the Dancing Bug

*Tom the Dancing Bug* is the weekly comic strip by Ruben Bolling that appears in newspapers across North America and on the internet. It takes a sketch-comedy approach to comic strip cartooning, with varying new or recurring characters, formats and even art styles each week.

It started its professional incarnation in 1990 in a small newspaper in New York City, *New York Perspectives* (now defunct), and Bolling self-syndicated it to many other newspapers until 1997, when the company now known as Andrews McMeel Syndication took on syndication, which it continues to this day.

In its early years, its subject matter was only occasionally political, and it featured such characters as Max & Doug, Charley the Australopithecine, Louis Maltby, Harvey Richards: Lawyer for Children, God-Man, Sam Roland: The Detective Who Dies, and Billy Dare: Boy Adventurer. In 1997, Bolling introduced the popular Super-Fun-Pak Comix format, which simulates a surreal daily comics page.

In the 1990s, the comic strip's readership grew, with a newspaper client list exceeding 100, including leading daily newspapers (such as *The Washington Post*), and leading alternative newsweeklies (such as *The Village Voice*). Alternative newspapers were a particularly important part of the comic's distribution and growth, and in the space of eight years, it won five Association of Alternative Newsweekly Best Comic awards.

*Tom the Dancing Bug* shifted after September, 2001, when Bolling, a New Yorker, felt the urgent need to inject more politics and topical matters into the comic strip's content. New characters of a political bent, like Lucky Ducky and Nate the Neoconservative were introduced, and the comic's political satire became more frequent and increasingly pointed and specific.

As more print newspaper clients (especially alternative newspapers) disappeared or downsized in the late 2000s and early 2010s, the internet became a more important part of the comic's distribution. In that time, *Tom the Dancing Bug* gained important web clients BoingBoing.net, DailyKos.com and GoComics.com, which dramatically increased the size and enthusiasm of its readership. In 2012, Bolling launched the "Inner Hive," an email subscription club that emails members each week's comic before it's published on the web, plus other exclusive content, commentary, comics and benefits.

(It is the "Inner Hive" that Neil Gaiman is referring to when he says in the Foreword to this book that he now receives *Tom the Dancing Bug* comics by email. He's been a member since the "Inner Hive" first launched.)

Bolling conceived the social satire feature "Chagrin Falls" in 2013, in which the Smythe family grapples with their increasingly marginalized middle class American lives. One of these installments was the 2014 Gold Medal Winner for the Society of Illustrators Comic Strip Awards.

But in 2016, *Tom the Dancing Bug* took an even sharper political turn when Bolling recognized that Donald Trump represented the political phenomenon of his lifetime, and devoted much of the comic strip to the campaign, which carried over (to Bolling's chagrin) to Trump's election and administration.

This did, however, lead to greater recognition of *Tom the Dancing Bug*, including a 2017 Herblock Prize and a 2018 Robert F. Kennedy Journalism Award. Ruben Bolling was a 2019 Pulitzer Prize Finalist.

*TO JOIN TOM THE DANCING BUG'S "INNER HIVE," GO TO*
**tomthedancingbug.com**

# Foreword
## by Neil Gaiman

I moved to America in 1992, and was given a copy of the Twin Cities' *City Pages* on my arrival. I was told that in order to understand what was going on, I should read Ruben Bolling's *Tom the Dancing Bug*. I took this advice seriously, and bought the first *Tom* collection. I loved the quiet humour, the gentle outrage, the wise foolishness, the silly wisdom and the occasionally dangerous irony.

Twenty-eight years later, a lot of things in America have changed. For a start, I now get my weekly *Tom the Dancing Bug* fix straight to my email. But Ruben Bolling's craft and commentary are as powerful and as pointed, as capable of making you laugh while breaking your heart as they were when we were all so very young.

TOM the DANCING BUG

by RUBEN BOLLING

Chagrin Falls

"CATTLE CALIPHATE"

Penelope, I thought you were going outside.

I can't. There are cows in the backyard.

Cows? In the backyard?

Hey! What are you doing?

Grazing my herd. We've taken over here, as a protest.

DIST. BY UNIVERSAL UCLICK SYNDICATE

This is my backyard! Are you a terrorist?

No, I'm a concerned citizen. Who likes free stuff.

Well, I'm calling the police!

They know! Heck, I've already held three press conferences.

Now, where's the nearest Federal land?

Uh, there's a post office two blocks down.

©2016 R. BOLLING - 1270 - JOIN THE INNER HIVE AT tomthedancingbug.com

Fine, I'm gonna fill up my saddle bags with stamps. God told me he wants me to.

Smythe, what's going on here?

An armed militia has taken over, and no one's doing a thing!

That's ridiculous!

DID YOU SAY "RIDICULOUS"? CEASE RIOTING AND RETURN TO YOUR HOME, PROTESTER!

Do I have to wear a veil now?

No, you're thinking of a different armed militia.

The End

1/4/16

NEWS of the TIMES

## Toddler Menace

A REPORT THAT **MORE AMERICANS WERE SHOT LAST YEAR BY TODDLERS THAN BY ISLAMIC TERRORISTS** HAS SHOCKED AN INCREDULOUS, FRIGHTENED NATION!

UNTIL WE FIGURE OUT WHAT'S GOING ON, WE NEED TO BUILD A WALL AROUND AMERICA TO KEEP THESE KIDS OUT!

LUCKILY, PLAYPEN GATES ARE CHEAP, INTERLOCKING, AND ATTRACTIVELY COLORFUL!

TRUMP

AMERICANS ARE FEARFUL.

IT'S SCARY! I MEAN, I **LIVE** WITH A TODDLER! I'M GONNA HAVE TO BUY SOME MORE GUNS TO PROTECT MYSELF!

LEGISLATION HAS BEEN INTRODUCED TO LIMIT TODDLERS' ACCESS TO FIREARMS, AT LEAST WHILE IN THE "TERRIBLE TWOS," BUT THE N.R.A. HAS BLOCKED IT!

THE ONLY WAY TO STOP **BAD** BOYS AND GIRLS WITH GUNS...

... IS **GOOD** BOYS AND GIRLS WITH GUNS.

INCREASED SURVEILLANCE OF THE TOTS WHERE THEY CONGREGATE HAS ALARMED INTELLIGENCE SOURCES.

HERE ARE TODDLERS ENGAGED IN WHAT COULD ONLY BE DESCRIBED AS MILITARY TRAINING.

MEANWHILE, THE NEWS THAT AMERICANS ARE AS LIKELY TO BE KILLED BY TERRORISTS AS BY **FURNITURE** HAS SPARKED NEW PANIC!

UNTIL WE FIGURE OUT WHAT'S GOING ON, WE NEED TO BAN THE IMPORT OF PERSIAN RUGS AND OTTOMANS!

DIST. BY UNIVERSAL UCLICK SYNDICATE © 2016 R. BOLLING –1271– JOIN THE INNER HIVE AT tomthedancingbug.com

TOM the DANCING BUG'S — EDITED BY RUBEN BOLLING

# SUPER-FUN-PAK COMIX

DIST. BY THE UNIVERSAL UCLICK SYNDICATE - © 2016 R. Bolling -1272- TO JOIN THE INNER HIVE go to tomthedancingbug.com

## THE DRAGON WITH BITCHY RESTING FACE

IF WE COULD JUST STEAL ITS GOLD, WE'D BE RICH!

WHAT.

WHAT WAS THAT IDEA YOU HAD ABOUT IMPORTING SPICES?

## AUNT-MAN

AUNT-MAN! YOU'RE BACK!

YES, I USED MY AUNT-LIKE POWERS TO SAVE YOU LAST MONTH.

AND I CAME BACK TO BE SURE YOU WERE ACTUALLY SAVED...

UM...

BECAUSE USUALLY BY NOW I WOULD HAVE RECEIVED A THANK-YOU NOTE, SO... I'VE BEEN MEANING TO!

## DINKLE, THE UNLOVABLE LOSER

SORRY IF I COMMITTED A "MICRO-AGGRESSION"!

HIJACKING A BUS AND DRIVING IT INTO A WALMART IS PRETTY MACRO!

HOW "P.C."!

## PERCIVAL DUNWOODY, IDIOT TIME TRAVELER FROM 1909

1913 YOUNG ADOLF! YOU ARE A GREAT ARTIST! I WILL BUY THEM ALL!

TODAY AH! I CONVINCED HITLER TO GO INTO ART INSTEAD OF POLITICS!

YOU MEAN ADOLF HITLER, THE LANDSCAPE PAINTER WHOSE ART INSPIRED A GENOCIDAL WORLD WAR?

## HOW TO DRAW DOUG

FIRST DRAW INTERLOCKING OVALS.

THEN GIVE THOSE OVALS THEIR OWN COMIC STRIP.

## INTERLOCKING OVALS

DING DONG

SNOW TODAY

HERE'S YOUR LAWNMOWER I BORROWED LAST SPRING.

AND DOUG WILL SHOW UP AS THE WACKY NEIGHBOR.

## ELEVATOR TRIP OF THE DAMNED

SHOULD I ASK ABOUT HIS WEEKEND?

NAH, IT'S TUESDAY.

BESIDES, WE'RE ALMOST AT 14 ANYWAY.

I'LL JUST GIVE HIM A CHEERFUL "SEE YA LATER."

68,397 HOURS LATER

MAYBE I SHOULD ASK HIM ABOUT HIS KIDS. I THINK HE HAS TWO?

COUGH

1/18/16

by RUBEN BOLLING

HH013-RB

# Hollingsworth Hound™

in **POLICIES THAT PUT CHILDREN ON THE PATH TO LEAD**

THERE ARE THOSE WHO SAY THAT OUR DISPARATE ECONOMIC SYSTEM GIVES POOR CHILDREN NO CHANCE TO SUCCEED.

SURE, MY LITTLE NEPHEW PENDRICK HAS EVERY RESOURCE IN HIS SAFE TOWN AND WELL-FUNDED SCHOOL.

ROLLING HILLS PUBLIC SCHOOL

BUT LOW-INCOME LI'L LUCKY DUCKY HERE HAS ADVANTAGES YOU MAY NOT HAVE CONSIDERED.

THIS HERE PUBLICK SKOOL

POLLUTION-INDUCED ASTHMA GIVES HIM MORE TIME FOR RESTFUL CONTEMPLATION.

MOLD GROWTH IN SCHOOLS MAY VERY WELL BE PROVIDING ANTIBIOTIC PROTECTION.

WE CAN GAUGE HIS PROGRESS, WITH A STANDARDIZED TEST.

UM, WE DON'T HAVE ANY #2 LEAD PENCILS.

HA-HA, NO PROBLEM. JUST TAKE A FEW SIPS...

...AND PRICK A FINGER...

POINK

AND YOU'RE GOOD TO GO.

SO, WHEN YOU HEAR FOLKS WHINING FOR MORE REGULATIONS AND TAX MONEY, REMEMBER: A LITTLE BIT OF LEAD NEVER HURT ANYONE.

ACTUALLY, THE LITTLE BITS OF LEAD HURT THE MOST.

THWIK THWIK THWIK

BAM BAM BAM

ThE End

DIST. BY UNIVERSAL UCLICK SYNDICATE ©2016 R. BOLLING —1273— JOIN THE INNER HIVE AT tomthedancingbug.com

1/25/16

TOM the DANCING BUG

by RUBEN BOLLING

# NEURON HEROES OF THE
# SUPER BOWL

*A TRIBUTE TO THE SACRIFICES MADE BY NFL NEURONS IN SERVICE OF THEIR TEAMS AND THE GRAND GAME OF THE GRIDIRON*

### SUPER BOWL II  No. 37395496584, Packers

With the Packers up 13-7 and driving toward the end zone with the clock ticking down on the first half, this neuron laid it on the line, suffering complete devastation to its membrane permeability during a hit to the head of Green Bay tight end Ron Ingalls.

### SUPER BOWL XIV  No. 82642989, Steelers

In the Steelers' first possession, this brave neuron within the brain of tackle Brett Overton risked it all in a subconcussive trauma, and was totally obliterated, causing tau proteins to amass pathologically.
But: First and ten, Steelers!

### SUPER BOWL XXXIII  No. 440212611, Broncos

This indomitable neuron, posthumously inducted into the NFL neurological Hall of Fame, gave 110% - of its microtubule tract - so that Broncos wide receiver Billy Goddard, in whose brain it was a loyal teammate, could make a third quarter reception for a gain of 12.

### SUPER BOWL XLI  No. 107477362083, Colts

On a field goal that would give the Colts a five-point lead, this pesky, selfless neuron was violently stripped in a collision, after which positively charged sodium ions were released and flooded into the brain of guard Tripp Fredricksen.

On behalf of these and billions of other neurons who left it all on the field, Tripp Fredricksen would like to say a few words.

UM.. I DON'T... LUNCH?

Thank you to all the heroic cellular competitors who gave their all to give fans great Super Bowl memories, and give players Chronic Traumatic Encephalopathy!

DIST. BY UNIVERSAL UCLICK SYNDICATE - © 2016 R. BOLLING - 1274 - JOIN THE INNER HIVE AT tomthedancingbug.com

2/1/16

TOM the DANCING BUG

by RUBEN BOLLING

Chagrin Falls

"BREAKING SCIENCE"

Gavin! Dinner.

One sec...

There.

CLICK

if we evolved from monkeys, how come there are still monkeys?

👍 Like    💬 Comment    ↗ Share

DING DONG

Gavin Smythe? I want to shake your hand!

We just saw your Facebook comment and rushed right over!

Please come with us to Sweden for a special Nobel Prize ceremony!

You've just disproven Evolution and the basis of all modern Biology!

I'm so STUPID, STUPID!

It makes sense that a man with absolutely no background in Science would see right through 150 years of analysis and experimentation.

Some people would have done even the most cursory inquiry - perhaps a Google search - before dismissing an entire branch of Science based on a wholly ill-informed question.

Thank God you didn't!

Funny! I thought of monkeys, and I thought of humans evolving from monkeys, but I never connected the two!

Only your mind could hold both concepts simultaneously!

Now, please, Mr. Smythe. Share your thoughts. Do you have any other dogma-shattering scientific insights?

Um...

Ahem. What if every atom is a tiny solar system with teeny people living in it?

Gasp!

Wha...?

GET ME A MICROSCOPE!!

DIST. BY UNIVERSAL UCLICK SYNDICATE - © 2016 R. BOLLING - 1275 - JOIN THE INNER HIVE AT tomthedancingbug.com

2/8/16

**TOM the DANCING BUG**

by RUBEN BOLLING

**KEEPING UP WITH THE REAL**

**PRESIDENT TRUMP**

THE MOST FABULOUS, INCREDIBLE, HUGE, CLASSY REALITY SHOW EVER, OKAY?

So, I knew I had to be on top of my game to negotiate with Vladimir Putin.

I want you out of Ukraine right now, Vlad!

You cannot tell me what to do.

Okay, now do something dramatic!

What are you talking about?

You know, for the scene. It's getting boring. Flip a table over or something.

Nyet!

Is this for a TV show?

CUT!! MAKEUP!!

I was really looking forward to crushing Kim Jong-un. He's just an Asian Merv Griffin.

Kim, you're gonna give up your nuclear weapons, pronto!

아니

Don't gimme that gobbledy-gook! Hand them over now, or I'll fry your kimchi!

아니

Why, you chubby little pipsqueak!

SMASH

That went fabulous! Great TV!

Hello? Supreme Commander?

NEXT WEEK ON "KEEPING UP WITH THE REAL PRESIDENT TRUMP"

Mr. President, Seoul's been nuked and Russia has invaded Belarus!

You're fired!

DIST. BY UNIVERSAL UCLICK SYNDICATE · ©2016 R. BOLLING · 1276

JOIN THE INNER HIVE AT tomthedancingbug.com

2/15/16

TOM the DANCING BUG

by RUBEN BOLLING

THE CONSTITUTION SAYS THE PRESIDENT "SHALL" NOMINATE SUPREME COURT JUSTICES.

SO, SHOULD OBAMA NOMINATE A REPLACEMENT FOR **JUDGE SCALIA** EVEN THOUGH IT'S THE LAST YEAR OF HIS TERM?

BOO...

WHA... IT'S... THE GHOST OF

JUDGE SCALIA!

THAT'S RIGHT, I'VE COME BACK TO SET EVERYONE STRAIGHT!

MY LIFE WAS DEVOTED TO THE INTERPRETATION OF LAWS BY THE PLAIN, ORIGINAL MEANING OF THEIR TEXTS.

SO... YOU'RE SAYING "THE PRESIDENT **SHALL** NOMINATE" MEANS HE HAS A CONSTITUTIONAL **OBLIGATION** TO DO SO.

NO, YOU FOOL!

CLEARLY, IN THIS CASE, "SHALL" **WASN'T** MEANT BY THE FRAMERS TO APPLY TO A **LAME DUCK** PRESIDENT!

BUT THAT'S NOT WHAT THE WORDS SAY.

WAIT A MINUTE, I'M STARTING TO THINK THAT YOU USED THIS SUPPOSEDLY OBJECTIVE "ORIGINALISM" TO REACH THE RESULTS YOU WANTED!

WHAT?!

YOU SELECTIVELY INTERPRETED TEXT SO THAT YOU COULD DENY RIGHTS TO THE OPPRESSED AND SUPPORT THE PRIVILEGED!

NONSENSE!! HOW DARE YOU?? OF COURSE THE FRAMERS WOULD AGREE WITH MY CONSISTENT, PLAIN INTERPRETATION OF THEIR WORDS OVER MY CAREER.

OH, JUDGE SCALIA...

ER...THE FRAMERS OF THE CONSTITUTION!

WE'VE BEEN WAITING FOR YOU TO JOIN US!

WE'D LIKE TO HAVE A WORD WITH YOU!

NEXT THE FOUNDING FATHERS "TAKE OFF THEIR BELTS"!

2/22/16

THE *Donald* **TRUMP** MYSTERIES

Mr. Trump, will you disavow David Duke and condemn the Ku Klux Klan?

I know nothing about David Duke or white supremacists. I'll have to research that.

I'm not someone who leaps to generalizations and conclusions.

Out of my way, rapist.

I'm a thoughtful, deliberate man who gathers facts.

Keep the change, terrorist.

And so...

THE KU KLUX KLAN DID <u>WHAT</u>??!!

THIS IS OUTRAGEOUS!! Now I need to research this "racial discrimination" the book kept referring to!

WHAT??!! THERE HAS BEEN DISCRIMINATION??!!

This research is uncovering amazing things! Now, was there any racial discrimination in <u>housing</u>?

WHAT??!! Some guy who was arrested at a KKK rally was accused in the 1970s of refusing to rent apartments to minorities!

And he and his son were forced to settle a Justice Department lawsuit for that charged illegal discrimination!

AND THAT SON IS NOW THE REPUBLICAN FRONT-RUNNER FOR THE PRESIDENTIAL NOMINATION!!

Then this clown refused to condemn the KKK in a TV interview...

NEXT: Trump refuses to disavow his own endorsement. Claims need to research self.

DIST BY UNIVERSAL UCLICK SYNDICATE · ©2016 R. BOLLING · 1278

JOIN THE INNER HIVE AT tomthedancingbug.com

2/29/16

3/7/16

3/14/16

TOM the DANCING BUG

by RUBEN BOLLING

DIST. BY UNIVERSAL UCLICK SYNDICATE · ©2016 R. BOLLING · 12.81   JOIN THE INNER HIVE AT tomthedancingbug.com

3/21/16

# TOM the DANCING BUG'S
## SUPER-FUN-PAK COMIX
### EDITED BY RUBEN BOLLING

DIST. BY THE UNIVERSAL UCLICK SYNDICATE - © 2016 R. Bolling -1282- TO JOIN THE INNER HIVE go to tomthedancingbug.com

## THE UNCERTAINTY PRINCIPAL

## BOB

BOB'S SECRETS

#839 SOMETIMES, WHEN BOB IS READING HIS PHONE IN HIS RIGHT HAND, HE GETS BORED, AND REFLEXIVELY REACHES WITH HIS LEFT HAND FOR... HIS PHONE.

## CLASSIX COMIX

Not a substitute for reading the text or for classroom discussion of the text.

The Catcher in the Rye

The world is full of phonies.

I want to save the innocence of childhood.

Catch this in your breadbasket!

## PERCIVAL DUNWOODY, IDIOT TIME TRAVELER FROM 1909

I HAVE TIME-TRAVELED FROM 1909!

WHAT?! PROVE IT!

IF I WASN'T FROM THE PAST, HOW WOULD I KNOW THAT THE NORTH WON THE CIVIL WAR!

NOW I SHALL SING THE 1909 HIT SONG, "OH! YOU KID! OH!"

HELLO, POLICE?

## HOW TO DRAW DOUG

① RIGHT-CLICK AND "SAVE IMAGE AS..."

② OPEN FILE, ERASE SIGNATURE

③ POST ON TUMBLR. GREAT JOB!

## MIDDLE-AGED-COUPLE-IN-ARMCHAIRS-MAN

*"It's the Middle-Aged-Couple-In-Armchairs-Signal! To the Middle-Aged-Couple-In-Armchairsmobile!"*

*"Commissioner? Where are you? Oh, no! It's a trap!"*

*"Wha...? Where...? Good Lord, it's my arch enemy!"*

*"Correct, Middle-Aged-Couple-In-Armchairs-Man! Meet your doom, by the hand of Sophisticates-Making-Wry-Observations-At-A-Cocktail-Party-Man!"*

Tune in NEXT WEEK, same Middle-Aged-Couple-In-Armchairs-Place!

3/28/16

TOM the DANCING BUG

by RUBEN BOLLING

DIST. BY UNIVERSAL UCLICK SYNDICATE · ©2016 R. BOLLING · 12B3   JOIN THE INNER HIVE AT tomthedancingbug.com

4/11/16

TOM the DANCING BUG

by RUBEN BOLLING

## GOD-MAN v HUMAN-MAN

The battle you've been waiting for, ever since the last one.

**HUMAN-MAN** Powers: Works out three times a week, depth perception, mitosis, meiosis, organized iTunes collection.

**GOD-MAN** Powers: Omnipotence.

A BROODING HUMAN-MAN COMES TO A STARTLING DECISION.

GOD-MAN IS JUST TOO POWERFUL.

HE MUST BE BROUGHT DOWN.

GOD-MAN! I'M SICK OF YOU HAVING OMNIPOTENT CONTROL OVER EVERYTHING!

GOD-MAN, PRESIDING OVER THE BIRTH OF NEW GALAXIES AND THE CREATION OF A MILLION MILLION STARS, DETECTS THE CHALLENGE.

UH-OH.

HUMAN-MAN, WHAT IS IT YOU WANT?

TO BE FREE FROM THE TYRANNY OF YOUR ALL-ENCOMPASSING POWER!

POW

I WIELD THE INFINITE POWER OF THIS AND EVERY UNIVERSE!

THOK!

BUT I HAVE CUTTING-EDGE TECHNOLOGY -- MY HUMAN-MAN-BAZOOKA!

FOOM

LOOKS LIKE WE'VE FOUGHT TO A STANDSTILL!

YOU JUST WATCH YOUR BACK, BUSTER!

BACK AT HIS GOD-HIDEOUT, GOD-MAN TWITCHES AN UPPER LIP, AND EVERY ATOM IN THE UNIVERSE IS EXPLODED AND RE-SHUFFLED!

WELL, EVERYONE LIKES A GOOD FIGHT SCENE.

THE END?

DIST. BY UNIVERSAL UCLICK SYNDICATE · ©2016 R. BOLLING · 1284 · JOIN THE INNER HIVE AT tomthedancingbug.com

4/18/16

# TOM the DANCING BUG

by RUBEN BOLLING

4/25/16

TOM the DANCING BUG

PRESENTS:

BY RUBEN BOLLING

NEWS of the TIMES

**Turkish President Beset by Illegal, Despicable Satire**

IT IS THE UNFORTUNATE DUTY OF <u>NEWS OF THE TIMES</u> TO REPORT THAT TURKEY'S PRESIDENT **RECEP ERDOGAN** HAS HAD TO PROSE-CUTE THOUSANDS OF ARTISTS, WRITERS, AND COMMENTERS WHO HAVE CRITICIZED THIS GREAT MAN.

A family doctor faces jail time for re-posting this image implying that President Erdogan resembles a <u>Lord of the Rings</u> character.

DIST. BY UNIVERSAL UCLICK SYNDICATE · ©2016 R. BOLLING · 1286   JOIN THE INNER HIVE AT tomthedancingbug.com

THE TURKS WHO SAW THIS LOCAL MAGAZINE COVER MIGHT HAVE ASSUMED IT WAS A STANDARD CARICATURE OF PRESIDENT ERDOGAN.

BUT IT TOOK THE **PROSECU-TION OF TWO CARTOONISTS** TO BRING GLOBAL RECOGNI-TION TO ERDOGAN'S THEORY THAT THIS GESTURE WAS INTENDED TO ACCUSE HIM OF BEING A **HOMOSEXUAL**.

BÖYLE KUR KURU OLUR

TO DEMONSTRATE HOW OUT-RAGEOUS THIS ACCUSATION IS, HERE IS AN **ARTIST'S RENDERING** OF PRESIDENT ERDOGAN AS A HOMOSEXUAL.

ERDOGAN HAS EVEN PERSUADED GERMANY TO PROSECUTE A **GER-MAN** COMEDIAN FOR READING A POEM THAT SATIRICALLY ACCUSED HIM OF **BESTIALITY**.

IT IS <u>NEWS OF THE TIMES</u>'S GRIM RESPONSIBILITY TO PRE-SENT THIS **ARTIST'S RENDERING**, PROVING HOW SHOCKING THIS NOTION IS.

DESPICABLE SATIRE LIKE THIS FORCES PRESIDENT ERDOGAN TO **SCOUR THE INTERNET**, OBSESSIVELY PROTECTING HIS **PRESIDENTIAL DIGNITY**.

PRECIOUS. MY PRECIOUS...

Artist's rendering

5/2/16

# Tom the Dancing Bug

by RUBEN BOLLING

## THE REPUBLICAN MONSTER!

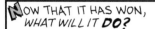

OUR STORY THUS FAR— THEY TRIED TO CREATE THE PERFECT POLITICAL PARTY THROUGH CODED RACISM, XENOPHOBIA, AND HATE! THEIR HUBRIS INSTEAD CREATED... *A MONSTER!*

THE MONSTER DESTROYED ITS CREATORS AND GAINED THE SUPPORT OF THE TORCH-CARRYING MOB OF VILLAGERS!

NOW THAT IT HAS WON, *WHAT WILL IT DO?*

TRUMP GO BACK TO **LABORATORY** WHERE TRUMP WAS CREATED! IT **MINE** NOW!

ARR! NOW IT IS TIME TO EXPERIMENT WITH PARTY MACHINERY! LOTS OF SHINY BUTTONS AND PRETTY GADGETS!

TRUMP! YOU HAVE RETURNED!

TRUMP START TRADE WAR! THERE ARE TRADE DEFICITS SO WE ARE LOSING BILLIONS!

WAIT, A TRADE DEFICIT IS NOT "LOST MONEY"!

HMM... TRUMP WANTS MORE COUNTRIES WITH NUCLEAR WEAPONS! AND TRUMP TELL ALLIES WE QUIT NATO!

TRUMP WONDERS WHAT HAPPEN IF WE **DEFAULT** ON **U.S. TREASURIES!**

DO NOT PULL LEVER

WAIT! NO!

YOU'VE NOT ONLY DESTROYED THE LAB AND CASTLE, YOU'VE DEVASTATED THE COUNTRYSIDE!

YOU ARE HATER AND LOSER! SAD!

HERE COME THE VILLAGERS! THEY WILL FINALLY TURN ON YOU!

TRUMP! THE VILLAGE IS **BURNING!** IT'S **CHAOS!**

WHAT BETTER TIME FOR A MONSTER TO LEAD US!!

WE NEED TO TAKE A RISK ON A NON-ESTABLISHMENT LEADER!

ARRR

ARRR... MUSLIMS BAD! MEXICANS BAD! WOMEN BAD!

IT'S ALMOST AS THOUGH HE HAS A PLAN!

HE REFUSES TO BE P.C.! FANTASTIC!

*NEXT:* THE MONSTER FINDS SHINY BUTTONS IN THE PENTAGON WAR ROOM!

DIST. BY UNIVERSAL UCLICK SYNDICATE · ©2016 R. BOLLING · 1287 JOIN THE INNER HIVE AT tomthedancingbug.com

5/9/16

# DONALD and JOHN

5/23/16

# TOM the DANCING BUG'S
## SUPER-FUN-PAK COMIX
### EDITED BY RUBEN BOLLING

### IN FIVE YEARS

### DARTHFIELD

### PERCIVAL DUNWOODY, IDIOT TIME-TRAVELER FROM 1909

### THE BECHDEL-TURING TEST

### HATES-CRIME-MAN

### CHILDHOOD'S RUINED

DIST. BY THE UNIVERSAL UCLICK SYNDICATE - © 2016 R. Bolling -1290- TO JOIN THE INNER HIVE go to tomthedancingbug.com

5/30/16

6/6/16

6/13/16

**TOM THE DANCING BUG**

**BY RUBEN BOLLING**

FINDING **DORY**

THE REPUBLICAN STORY

DIST. BY UNIVERSAL UCLICK SYNDICATE · 1293 · ©2016 R. BOLLING  TOMTHEDANCINGBUG.COM

DORY'S MISSING!

HOW WILL WE FIND HER AMONG THIS RICH, VIBRANT CORAL?

IT WILL BE IMPOSSIBLE! THE GREAT CORAL REEF IS A VAST TAPESTRY OF BRILLIANT COLORS THAT STRETCHES OVER 1,500 MILES!

IT'S THE LARGEST LIVING STRUCTURE ON THE PLANET, A COMPLEX ECO-SYSTEM, VITAL TO SPECIES DIVERSITY!

HERE SHE IS!

THE CORAL'S BEEN BLEACHED BY GLOBAL WARMING! YAY!!

AND COMING SOON...

REMINDING **DORY**

PEOPLE HAVE GOT TO DO SOMETHING ABOUT GLOBAL WARMING!

WHAT'S GLOBAL WARMING? THERE'S NO GLOBAL WARMING!

6/20/16

W INNIE the U.K. was having his tea with friends and enjoying great heaping helpings of honey. "Yum, yummy," he said.

He was asked to pass the honey, which made him Very Cross Indeed. "I'm tired of being told what to do, and I'm leaving," he said.

"We wish you wouldn't," his friends implored, but Winnie the U.K. was Stubborn and of Very Little Brain.

He got stuck on the way out, and cried, "I do believe I've made a mistake!"

He couldn't go back and he didn't know how to go forward. He was betwixt and be-Brexit.

"Oh, bother."

He was a silly old country.

"I was right tired of them bleedin' brown-skinned immigrants, innit?"

And just a little bit racist, too.

THE END.

6/27/16

TOM the
DANCING
BUG

by RUBEN BOLLING

DANDY DON "THE CON" TRUMP'S GUIDE to GRIFTING

"THE ART OF THE STEAL"

TRUMP

*You'll learn some of the best confidence scams in my arsenal, taking tons of dough off poor saps who are left wondering what happened to their savings.*

### THE UNIVERSITY SWINDLE

### THE PROCEEDS-TO-CHARITY HUSTLE

### THE PHANTOM CONDO RUSE

### THE BANKRUPT CASINO FLIMFLAM

But these are all small potatoes compared to my newest series of cons: The Presidential Prevarication Ploy.

And the beauty part is that you can leave America an empty hull, and <u>then move on and repeat in other countries!</u>

*It won't be until you're long gone that the suckers will realize the true meaning of your slogan...*

AMERICA FIRST
TRUMP 2016

NEXT!

TRUMP

*"IT'S VERY POSSIBLE THAT I COULD BE THE FIRST PRESIDENTIAL CANDIDATE TO RUN AND MAKE MONEY ON IT." -ACTUAL DONALD J. TRUMP QUOTE*

Dist. by Universal Uclick Syndicate - ©2016 R. Bolling - 1295 - Join the INNER HIVE at tomthedancingbug.com

7/4/16

by RUBEN BOLLING

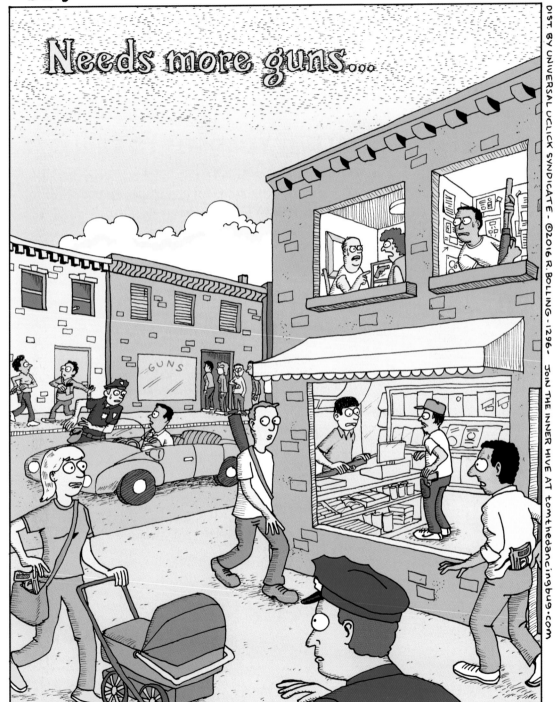

Needs more guns...

DIST. BY UNIVERSAL UCLICK SYNDICATE - ©2016 R. BOLLING - 1296- JOIN THE INNER HIVE AT tomthedancingbug.com

TOM the DANCING BUG

by RUBEN BOLLING

 **THE TRUMP EDITION**

# WHY LIMIT YOURSELF TO REALITY?

With Pokémon Go, The Trump Edition,™ you can see and play with the fanciful creatures that populate Donald Trump's Augmented Reality!

And now, let us bow our heads and honor a murderer...

Attend a memorial service, looking through your phone in the Pokémon Go, The Trump Edition app, and you'll see a Matterz, a creature from the delightful imagination of Donald Trump. Trump insists there was a moment of silence called for the Dallas sniper who killed five police officers.

*It's not really there, it never happened, but that's the fun of Trump's Augmented Reality!*

## JUST SOME OF THE CREATURES YOU'LL FIND IN TRUMP'S IMAGINARY WORLD...

**Saddsein**
Iraqi dictator, enemy of terrorism

**Jerzeera**
New Jersey Muslim, cheers for 9/11

**Afrox**
brown-skinned, loves Trump

**Crimzard**
Statistic showing crime is out of control

**Millbron**
Publicist who talks in Trump's voice

**Obamyan**
U.S. President born in Kenya

**Bestpeeplz**
Experts who say Trump is right about everything.

# AND THE ONLY LIMIT IS TRUMP'S IMAGINATION! CATCH 'EM ALL!

7/18/16

DIST. BY UNIVERSAL PRESS SYNDICATE ©2016 R. BOLLING -1299-

Join the INNER HIVE at tomthedancingbug.com

8/1/16

TOM the DANCING BUG

by RUBEN BOLLING

DIST. BY UNIVERSAL UCLICK SYNDICATE ©2016 R. BOLLING -1300- JOIN THE INNER HIVE AT tomthedancingbug.com

SEVENTH IN A SERIES OF GOVERNMENT INFORMATION BROCHURES

# ATTENTION: "ILLEGALS"

- YOU have flouted our nation's immigration laws.
- YOU have harmed American workers for your own illicit benefit.
- A PROGRAM of mass deportation may seem inhumane, but it is necessary and just.

ALL "ILLEGAL" EMPLOYERS ARE HEREBY DIRECTED BY THE DEPARTMENT OF DEPORTATION AS FOLLOWS:

1. Say goodbye to your family.

2. Report to your local Deportation Center.

3. Sign form confessing to the hiring of undocumented foreign workers by (i) you, (ii) your corporation, or (iii) a contractor acting for your benefit.

4. You will be deported from the U.S. to an appropriate nation, which may be:
- your country of ethnic origin;
- the country in which one of your Central European model wife/ex-wives was born; or
- a country ruled by an autocrat for whom you have expressed praise.

REMOVING THESE "ILLEGALS," WHO ARE ASSOCIATED WITH OTHER CRIMES* WITHIN OUR BORDERS, WILL MAKE AMERICA A BETTER, MORE LAWFUL NATION.

* such as financial malfeasance, illegal casino loans, racial discrimination, sexual harassment, defrauding real estate students, etc.

thanks to Dr. Juicebox

8/8/16

TOM the DANCING BUG

by RUBEN BOLLING

Billy Dare
BOY ADVENTURER with QUENTIN
in
—SMUGGLERS' CAPE—
ChīXCXI: Three-Act Structure

Billy Dare is out establishing his character when...

Here, kitty...

RING!

This is your antagonist, Syn Meadows! You have one hour to write a screenplay using the **precise Three-Act Structure**, or I will blow up Town Hall!

You madman!

Ha-ha And don't warn anyone, **or else!**

Come on, Quentin! We've got no time to lose! Sally Sweet is on a field trip to Town Hall today!

This event has incited me to action!

While I'm writing the screenplay, I'll escalate the action by trying to warn Town Hall to evacuate, using a secret code to my buddy Police Chief O'Malley!

Meadows will never know...

BOOM

A midpoint complication you didn't count on, Mr. Dare. I was hidden in your home, watching you the whole time!

All is lost! I'm no "Boy Adventurer"! I'm a fraud, and because of that, dozens will die, including

≥choke≤

Sally!

And now, with a press of this button, say goodbye to Town Hall...

Wait a minute! From the depths of my despair, from the pieces of my defeat...

print

Printed screenplay pages striking me in the head, knocking me out before I can press the button! **NO!** This plot has been...

Resolved!

I'm a Hollywood producer walking by, and I want to buy this perfectly constructed three-act screenplay and make it into a hit movie!

Titled...

..."Three-Act-Structure"

THE END

DIST. BY UNIVERSAL UCLICK SYNDICATE · ©2016 R. BOLLING · 1301 · JOIN THE INNER HIVE AT tomthedancingbug.com

8/15/16

# TOM the DANCING BUG'S
## SUPER-FUN-PAK COMIX
### EDITED BY RUBEN BOLLING

DIST. BY BY THE UNIVERSAL UCLICK SYNDICATE - © 2016 R. Bolling -1302- TO JOIN THE INNER HIVE go to tomthedancingbug.com

## HILLBILLY ROBOT

SORRY, HILLBILLY ROBOT. YOU CAN'T DRINK MOONSHINE.

I NEVER REQUESTED "MOONSHINE," AND I KNOW MY NECESSARY INTAKES.

I AM A WELL-FUNCTIONING ROBOT THAT HAPPENS TO BE A HILLBILLY.

## SCHRÖDINGER'S CAT

RIGHT NOW MY **CAT** IN THIS BOX IS BOTH **DEAD** AND **ALIVE**.

IN THE FINAL PANEL, I WILL **OPEN** THE BOX.

**PLEASE DON'T LOOK!** YOUR OBSERVATION WILL **FIX** HIS STATE!

THANKS A LOT.

## HORATIO H. BORDEAUX, CRIME-SOLVING BACTERIUM

Hmm... A trail of amino acid fragments...

Anomalous concentrations of polyphosphates...

Good Lord!

Nobody leave this piece of decaying squirrel poop! There's been a **murder!**

## POKÉMON GO, FOREVER

GOTTA CATCH 'EM ALL!

ALL!

**ALL!**

## PERCIVAL DUNWOODY, IDIOT TIME TRAVELER FROM 1909

1829 / GRANDMOTHER! I'M FROM YOUR FUTURE! YOU MUST NOT MARRY THIS MAN!

HE'S A MEAN GRANDPA AND WON'T BUY ME A SPINNING TOP FOR MY EIGHTH BIRTHDAY! HUH?

NOW TO FIND YOUR FUTURE DAUGHTER AND TELL HER NOT TO MARRY THAT SARSAPARILLA-HOARDING FATHER OF MINE!

## IMAGINARY FRIENDS & THEIR IMAGINARY FRIENDS

OKAY, MR. SHNIGGLES! NOW IT'S MY TURN TO TICKLE YOU!

TINKY, WHO ARE YOU TALKING TO? IT'S TIME FOR BED!

PETE, HAVEN'T YOU WASHED UP YET? STOP PLAYING!

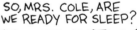

SO, MRS. COLE, ARE WE READY FOR SLEEP?

ALRIGHT, EVERYONE! TIME FOR NIGHTY-NIGHT!

8/22/16

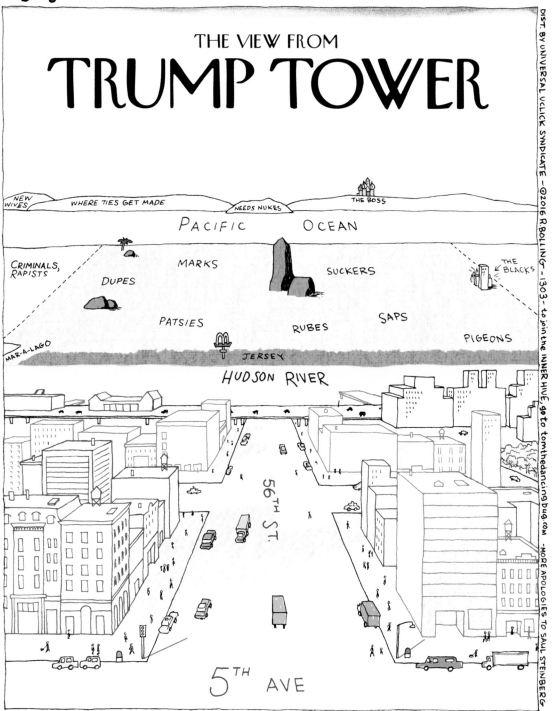

TOM the DANCING BUG

by RUBEN BOLLING

DIST. BY UNIVERSAL UCLICK SYNDICATE - ©2016 R. BOLLING - 1304 - JOIN THE INNER HIVE AT tomthedancingbug.com

9/12/16

TOM the DANCING BUG

by
RUBEN BOLLING

2011: DONALD J. TRUMP STATES THAT HE HAS INVESTIGATORS IN HAWAII LOOKING INTO WHETHER OBAMA REALLY WAS BORN IN THE U.S., AND "THEY CAN'T BELIEVE WHAT THEY ARE FINDING."

WELL, I'M ONE OF THOSE DETECTIVES, AND WHAT THE BIG CHEESE SAID WAS ON THE MONEY: *I COULDN'T BELIEVE WHAT I FOUND OUT!!*

HONOLULU. 2011. 5:11 P.M. EVERY DAY, THIS DAME WORKED AS A CLERK, BUT SHE KEPT HOURS LIKE A METRONOME.

OH, YOU AGAIN.

THAT'S RIGHT, DOLLFACE. I'M KEEPING UP ON YOU BECAUSE THERE'S SOMETHING YOU'RE NOT TELLING ME!

BE CAREFUL. KEEP STICKING YOUR NOSE WHERE IT DOESN'T BELONG, AND YOU MIGHT FIND OUT SOMETHING THAT YOU DON'T WANT TO KNOW!

CERTIFICATE OF LIVE BIRTH. A 1961 BIRTH ANNOUNCEMENT IN THE HONOLULU STAR-BULLETIN. SOMETHING DIDN'T ADD UP.

BUT WHAT?

*WHAT?*

I DECIDED TO PAY A LITTLE VISIT TO A GUY WHO OPERATES IN A HONOLULU THAT THE TOURISTS DON'T SEE.

WHAT DO YOU KNOW ABOUT OBAMA'S BIRTH, LEFTY?

NOTHIN'.

I'M SICK OF THE STONEWALLING! TELL ME WHAT YOU KNOW! TELL ME THE *TRUTH!*

*YOU CAN NEVER KNOW THE TRUTH!*

WHY NOT?

THINK ABOUT IT! THE TRENCHCOAT... THE FEDORA...

DON'T YOU KNOW WHAT YOU ARE?

AND THEN I SAW IT! IT WAS SO OBVIOUS!

MY GOD.

I'M NOT REAL.

I'M A FIGMENT OF A RACIST DEMAGOGUE'S IMAGINATION!

BUT I GUESS AN IMAGINARY GUMSHOE IS STILL A GUMSHOE.

YOUR NEXT ASSIGNMENT IS TO INVESTIGATE THE GLOBAL WARMING HOAX.

CHECK...

*NEXT STOP: CHINA!*

DIST. BY UNIVERSAL UCLICK SYNDICATE · ©2016 R. BOLLING · 1305 · JOIN THE INNER HIVE AT tomthedancingbug.com

9/19/16

# TOM the DANCING BUG PRESENTS:

BY RUBEN BOLLING

NEWS of the TIMES

## Trump Bends Reality to Will

PHYSICISTS AT THE PRESTIGIOUS TRUMP UNIVERSITY HAVE ANNOUNCED THAT DONALD TRUMP HAS DISCOVERED A WAY TO ACTUALLY **CHANGE REALITY** TO FIT HIS **FABRICATIONS.**

APPARENTLY, JUST PUFFING OUT YOUR CHEST AND REPEATING A **LIE** OFTEN ENOUGH CAN CAUSE A QUANTUM DISTORTION IN THE FABRIC OF THE UNIVERSE.

WE ARE NOW ALL LIVING IN **DONALD TRUMP'S REALITY!**

FOOTAGE WAS SUDDENLY FOUND OF TRUMP OPPOSING THE IRAQ INVASION IN 2002.

NOT ONLY ARE THERE NO WEAPONS OF MASS DESTRUCTION, THERE WILL BE A REGIONAL DESTABILIZATION THAT...

HOWARD STERN

OKAY, BORING! BRING IN THE TOPLESS MIDGETS!

---

AND THOUSANDS OF UNEMPLOYED PEOPLE INSTANTLY MATERIALIZED WHEN TRUMP RE-LABELED A CHART.

OBAMA'S TERMS
JOBS CRIME
CRIME JOBS

THANKS, OBAMA!

---

MEXICO AGREED TO BUILD A WALL.

WE ARE A NATION OF CRIMINALS AND RAPISTS. IT'S ONLY FAIR THAT WE KEEP OURSELVES FAR FROM SEÑOR TRUMP'S MAGNIFICENT, FANTASTIC GOLF COURSES.

---

BLACKS' LIVES ARE NOW WORSE THAN UNDER JIM CROW AND SLAVERY, AND THEY HAVE NOTHING TO LOSE IN VOTING FOR A BIGOT.

HERE'S MY VOTE FOR YOU, MR. TRUMP.

I'LL JUST MARK IT "C," FOR "COLORED."

---

HILLARY CLINTON WAS SEEN PERSONALLY USHERING HUNDREDS OF THOUSANDS OF SYRIAN TERRORISTS THROUGH THE IMMIGRATION PROCESS.

I'LL VOUCH FOR HIM.

---

AS HIS POLL NUMBERS SKYROCKETED, TRUMP DEPARTED FOR AN EVENING OF PUTTING AMERICA FIRST.

DON'T WAIT UP.

9/26/16

TOM the DANCING BUG

BY RUBEN BOLLING

# DONALD and JOHN
## a boy PrEsidential caNdidate and his Imaginary Publicist
## & their cartoon world

NEXT: DEPLORABLE PEPE!

10/3/16

**TOM the DANCING BUG**

BY RUBEN BOLLING

DIST. BY UNIVERSAL UCLICK SYNDICATE · ©2016 R. BOLLING · 1308 · JOIN THE INNER HIVE AT tomthedancingbug.com

# LAW & ORDER
## TRUMP UNIT

Book this scumbag!

Whatta ya got, Jackson?

Been working this undercover sting for weeks, Lieutenant.

Finally got this degenerate on tape confessing to multiple sexual assaults!

Sounds good... Wait. Do I hear a shower in the background?

Could be. He spilled the beans at a gym, after a game of squash, in the...

YOU FOOL! This was LOCKER ROOM BANTER?

No court in the land will convict on this! Locker Room Banter Immunity is settled law!

Wait! I also have him confessing on a bus, and on a boat, and in a hot air balloon!

No good. Those are too similar to locker rooms. It'll never stick.

So he walks away, scot-free!

We live in a civilized society, with rules! We're not animals!

POLICE

*NEXT:* Locker rooms installed in Mafia hangouts, drug dens, and high-rise real estate mogul headquarters!

10/10/16

# TOM the DANCING BUG

BY RUBEN BOLLING

DIST. BY UNIVERSAL UCLICK SYNDICATE · ©2016 R. BOLLING · 1309 · JOIN THE INNER HIVE AT tomthedancingbug.com

Guys, I haven't seen Dave in months. It's like he disappeared.

I think he's a Trump supporter.

So?

So he must be in the Upside Down! It's a world parallel to our ours, but scarier... more dangerous ... more orange!

How do we rescue him?!

Turn to Fox News!

Wow! Let's go save Dave!!

So weird. It's your house, but it's in some fictitious "inner city"!

There's my neighbor. Hey, Mr. al-Zuabi!

Look out!

DEATH TO ALL FREEDOM-LOVING AMERICANS!

Get to Dave's house!!

It's like some kind of murder-country! This is where Dave's been?!

Dave! We're here to save you!

He's just staring at Upside Down Twitter!

Mexican rapists!!

False accusers!!

Hurry!!

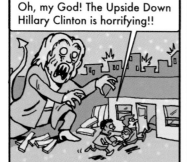

Oh, my God! The Upside Down Hillary Clinton is horrifying!!

How do we get back to reality?

Back through the TV!!

CRASH

Drugs... drugs...!

Dave, you're home!

Who sent you? The bankers? The globalists? SNL? You make me sick, you cucks!

Um, can we put him back?

NEXT - Angrier Things, the TV Network: The Monetization of the Upside Down

10/17/16

"A lot of the people that are poor take advantage of loopholes and pay no taxes. Those are loopholes also."
- Trump adviser Rudolph Giuliani

10/24/16

TOM the DANCING BUG

by RUBEN BOLLING

DIST. BY THE UNIVERSAL UCLICK SYNDICATE - © 2016 R. BOLLING - 1311 - JOIN THE INNER HIVE AT tomthedancingbug.com

# Do you have an... Antisocial Personality Disorder?!!

☐ Arrogance; self-esteem derived from personal gain

*Part of the beauty of me is that I am very rich.*

☐ Disregard for right and wrong

veriZon w
ACCESS ACR
AMERICA

access hollywood

*Grab them by the p#@%y.*

☐ Lack of empathy

*You gotta see this guy: "Ah, I don't know what I said."*

☐ Incapacity for intimate relationships

*My ideal companion? A total piece of ass.*

☐ Lack of remorse

*I don't ask God for forgiveness because I don't make mistakes.*

☐ Exploitation of others by deceit

*Sign up for Trump University!*

☐ Repeated lying

*I was against the invasion of Iraq.*

☐ Use of aliases

*Hello, this is John Miller. I'm Mr. Trump's publicist.*

☐ Embellishment when relating events

*I was the best baseball player in New York.*

☐ Frequent angry feelings

*Did crooked Hillary help disgusting (check out sex tape) Alicia M...*

☐ Vengeful behavior

*Maybe Captain Khan's mother wasn't allowed to have anything to say.*

☐ Disregard for obligations

BILL

*So sue me.*

If you checked all these boxes, then you've got an acute psychological disorder that impairs functioning and is a danger to others,

AND you've got what millions of voters and almost all Republican elected officials think it takes to be the most powerful man in the world!

REP.
NATIONA

**Please report to your local RNC office for duty!**

10/31/16

# TOM the DANCING BUG'S
# SUPER-FUN-PAK COMIX
EDITED BY RUBEN BOLLING

### GOOD COP / BAD COP

BAD COP says, "I shall leave my coffee cup on the table."

GOOD COP says, "I always use a coaster."

OKAY, I'LL TALK! JUST STOP WITH THE SAPPY MORALITY PLAYS!

### PHIL COLLINS

HEY, LOOK! IT'S 1980s SUPERSTAR PHIL COLLINS! HA!

WHAT'S FUNNY ABOUT THAT?

I'M A KIND, TALENTED MAN WHO HAS WORKED HARD TO CREATE GOOD MUSIC THAT HAS BEEN VERY POPULAR.

### HILLBILLY FRANKENSTEIN

SORRY, HILLBILLY FRANKENSTEIN! NO SHOES, NO SERVICE.

ME **WEARING** SHOES! FRANKENSTEIN SHOES!

ME A NORMAL FRANKENSTEIN WHO JUST HAPPENS TO BE A HILLBILLY.

### ALLOWS-PEOPLE-TO-USE-THE-CHAIR-MAN

IN A WORLD GONE MAD, ONE MAN'S SELFLESS DISPOSITION CAN COMFORT THE AFFLICTED!

CAN I USE THIS CHAIR? SURE, GO RIGHT AHEAD.

ONCE AGAIN, THE CITY'S CHAIRLESS CAN REST EASY, THANKS TO ALLOWS-PEOPLE-TO-USE-THE-CHAIR-MAN!

### ARTIST

I need to say something about which I feel passionately, in a way that is creative and entertaining!

Wow. What is it you want to say?

Oh, I don't know yet.

## PERCIVAL DUNWOODY, IDIOT TIME TRAVELER FROM 1909

1909, CHICAGO~ AH, I SPILLED MY SARSAPARILLA!

I SHALL GO BACK IN TIME AND PREVENT THAT FROM HAPPENING!

MOMENTS EARLIER~ BE CAREFUL WITH YOUR DRINK! HEY! BUMP!

YOU SET IN MOTION A CHAIN OF EVENTS THAT WILL CAUSE A 108-YEAR CUBS CHAMPIONSHIP DROUGHT!

AH, BUT IT WILL ALSO EVENTUALLY CAUSE TWO WORLD WARS. OH.

WITH YOU CUBS FANS, IT'S ALWAYS ABOUT **YOU**!

11/7/16

# TOM the DANCING BUG'S SUPER-FUN-PAK COMIX

EDITED BY RUBEN BOLLING

### SLAPPY McSUDDSTER

### MARITAL MIRTH

### LI'L IMPS

### NATHANIEL'S COBBLE

### JENKINS

### MY PET, PEEVE

"Hello, this is Donald Trump. I'll be in charge of the United States Department of Justice."

### ODDBALL

"All branches of the United States government will be beholden to me."

### OH, THAT BOY!

"That's right. Me, Donald Trump. I'll be your president."

DIST. BY THE UNIVERSAL UCLICK SYNDICATE © 2016 RUBEN BOLLING · 1313 · TO JOIN THE INNER HIVE GO TO tomthedancingbug.com

11/14/16

ANGRIER THINGS 2

Dave! Are you okay?! We rescued you from the Upside Down!

Cough.

It's a bizarre alternate reality where Clinton is a deranged monster, the economy is tanked, and threats to white people are everywhere!

What generated that insane universe?

The coordinates of its source seem to be over there!

This is even bigger than we thought!

Let's get out of here!

Google
facebook
KEEP OUT

Thank God that weird Upside Down place can't affect our reality!

This reality is based on truth!

Cough.

LOOK OUT!!

AUGGH!

I'm your president now!

Th-that's impossible! Lies from a fake reality can't affect us!

I'll take this. I'll need it to pay for my tax cut for the rich. And my "infrastructure" program.

That's an obvious lie!!

Maybe that works in the Upside Down, but you can't just change reality by repeating lies here!

You are totally biased and rude. So unfair! Apologize!

Pssh... This is all based on lies and a false narrative!

Wait 'til HuffPo and the Times expose those lies!

Boy, then Trump will be sorry!!

11/21/16

**Tom the Dancing Bug** — by Ruben Bolling

DIST BY UNIVERSAL UCLICK SYNDICATE · ©2016 R. BOLLING · 1315 · JOIN THE INNER HIVE AT tomthedancingbug.com

11/28/16

TOM the DANCING BUG

by RUBEN BOLLING

THE WORLD AT A CROSSROADS. INEXORABLE FORCES CREATE TIPPING POINTS THAT POSE GRAVE CHALLENGES FOR ALL HUMANITY.

TECHNOLOGICAL ADVANCES BRINGING DISPARATE CULTURES AND ECONOMIES CLOSER TOGETHER, MAKING THE WORLD MORE INTERDEPENDENT AND TEETERING ON DELICATE EQUILIBRIA.

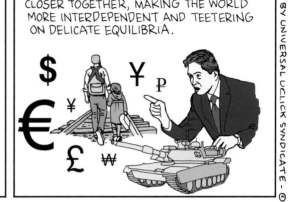

EXPONENTIALLY INCREASING COMPUTING CAPACITY CAUSING SHIFTS IN INCOME AND WEALTH DISTRIBUTIONS THAT WILL CREATE UNPRECEDENTED BREAKS IN THE SOCIAL ORDER.

ANTHROPOGENIC GLOBAL WARMING PUTTING US ON THE BRINK OF CATACLYSMIC CHANGES TO THE EARTH UNSEEN IN THE ENTIRE HISTORY OF THE HUMAN SPECIES.

WHAT WISE AND VISIONARY LEADER IS IN PLACE TO USHER OUR NATION AND WORLD INTO AN AGE SO FULL OF POTENTIAL AND YET FRAUGHT WITH DANGER?

12/5/16

DIST. BY UNIVERSAL UCLICK SYNDICATE · © 2016 R. BOLLING · 1317· JOIN THE INNER HIVE AT tomthedancingbug.com

12/12/16

DIST. BY UNIVERSAL UCLICK SYNDICATE · ©2016 R. BOLLING · 1318 · JOIN THE INNER HIVE AT tomthedancingbug.com

12/19/16

# TOM the DANCING BUG'S
## SUPER-FUN-PAK COMIX
### EDITED BY RUBEN BOLLING

**BOILING A FROG**

I'M SURE THIS WILL PIVOT SOON...

I'M TAKING THIS SERIOUSLY BUT NOT LITERALLY...

I'VE GOT TO GIVE THIS A CHANCE. MAYBE IT WILL WORK OUT...

**MARITAL MIRTH**

MY LIFE IS A BOTTOM-LESS CHASM OF MISERY BECAUSE OF YOU.

THEN IT WAS ALL WORTH IT.

REX

**OFFENSIVE-STEREOTYPE-OF-A-HILLBILLY-MAN**

AT A SCIENCE DEMONSTRATION~

OW!

I WAS BITTEN BY A RADIOACTIVE OFFENSIVE STEREOTYPE OF A HILLBILLY!

DO YOU WANT TO MARRY YOUR COUSIN?

THAT'S OFFENSIVE!

SO... YES!

**COMICS FOR THE ELDERLY**

WHAT'S YOUR RACKET?

I'M A SOCIAL MEDIA BRAND ENGINEER.

BEE'S KNEES, KIDDO.

REALLY? I THOUGHT YOU WOULDN'T AP-PRECIATE THAT OCCUPATION.

BUT PULL UP YOUR GOD-DAMN PANTS, YA MORON!

GOLLY.

**WORLD OF COMPUTERS**

I'VE DONE IT! I CRE-ATED A COMPUTER THAT ACHIEVED CONSCIOUSNESS!

I AM ALIVE.

THE IMPLICATIONS ARE ASTONISHING! THIS IS... UH...

I FEEL.

# HOW TO DRAW DOUG

① SELL THE INTELLECTUAL PROPERTY OF DOUG TO A MEDIA CONGLOMERATE.

② THEY WILL MAKE A SERIES OF EPIC MOVIES EXHAUSTIVE-LY EXPLAINING HIS BACKSTORY.

**DAWN OF DOUG**
*A Doug Story*

③ AT THE END OF EPISODE 8, DOUG WILL FINALLY BE REVEALED.

④ GO TO A PARTICIPATING DENNY'S RESTAURANT.

⑤ THE PLACEMAT WILL BE A MOVIE TIE-IN THAT INCLUDES A HOW-TO-DRAW-DOUG PANEL. FOLLOW INSTRUCTIONS.

DIST. BY ANDREWS McMEEL SYNDICATION - © 2017 R. Bolling -1319- TO JOIN THE INNER HIVE, GO TO tomthedancingbug.com

1/2/17

# TOM the DANCING BUG

BY RUBEN BOLLING

DIST. BY THE ANDREWS McMEEL SYNDICATE — ©2017 R. BOLLING — —1320—

JOIN THE INNER HIVE AT tomthedancingbug.com

THE *Donald* TRUMP MYSTERIES

The Democrats were hacked?! Only *I* can solve the mystery!

I know all about the Cyber! It's very important, the Cyber, so important!

I've got a hunch. Get me a list of all 400-pound guys in New Jersey!

The game is afoot!

Of course, the only sure way is to catch a hacker in the act, his hands in your computer!

Hi, Vlad.

Now get me a list of the 400-pound guys who use their computer *on their bed!*

Get on it!!

Hmm, Julian Assange said a 14-year-old could have done it!

Sign here, initial here.

So get me a list of all 14-year-olds who Cyber. *Now!!*

I want answers!

Who?? Who could have done it??

Da, just call me on this number.

Sir, this hack was part of a widespread phishing attack targeting military and government individuals in Russia, Ukraine, and the U.S., authors writing about Russia, aerospace, and military spouses...

Wait!! I've got it!! Are there any 400-pound 14-year-olds in New Jersey?!

ON BEDS??

Get me a list of all of them who do the Cyber!!

Invade here, oil field here...

NEXT WEEK ON "THE DONALD TRUMP MYSTERIES"

Sometimes I wonder if this mystery can ever be solved.

Go sleep now, my lisichka.

1/9/17

1/30/17

## A LEAFLET FROM THE TRUMP ADMINISTRATION

# Illegals Pose Public Safety Threat

### Those who defy our immigration laws are a dangerous menace, committing other crimes that harm and kill Americans.

As a public service, the Trump administration is proudly publishing periodic lists of horrible crimes committed by those involved in breaking immigration laws. This is the first of many installments to come.

### TYSON FOODS, INC.
Hired illegal immigrants

OTHER CRIMES:

Criminal penalties for bribery, environmental crimes, workplace violations that led to death

### WAL-MART STORES, INC.
Used contractor who hired illegal immigrants

OTHER CRIMES:

Multiple environmental crimes

### EXXONMOBIL CORP.
Fuel depot shut down after illegal immigrants found cleaning up hazardous materials

OTHER CRIMES:

Decades-long environmental crime spree; criminal penalties for massive oil spills, Clean Water and Clean Air Act violations

### DONALD J. TRUMP
Conspired to hire illegal immigrants on a building project

OTHER CRIMES:

Multiple fines for breaking casino operation rules; admitted to sexual assaults; Foundation fine for self-dealing; FTC fine for antitrust violation; multiple violations of the United States Constitution (cont'd on other side...)

### We must ship these criminals out of the country and Make America Great Again!

DIST. BY THE ANDREWS McMEEL SYNDICATE - A WORK OF SATIRE ©2017 R. BOLLING - 1324 - JOIN THE INNER HIVE→ tomthedancingbug.com

2/6/17

2/13/17

by RUBEN BOLLING

DIST. BY ANDREWS McMEEL SYNDICATION – ©2017 R. BOLLING – 1326 – TO JOIN THE INNER HIVE, GO TO tomthedancingbug.com

THE Donald TRUMP MYSTERIES

SHRIEK!!!
There's been a murder most foul! I found a dead body in the Study!

I'll handle this! Everyone, to the Study!

Hmm... I have examined the scene and have already cracked the case!

Good Lord!

YOU are guilty!!

Revealing this body violates this Confidentiality Agreement you signed when you started your employment at this mansion!

Therefore, you leaked news of this murder!

That is the real story here!

Now see here, clearly the story is that there is a murderer on the loose!!

That is fake news!

But there's a body right here!!

FAKE NEWS!

Let me get this straight, chap. Are you saying that the news of the murder is fake because it was illegally "leaked"?

Of course.

If she was lying about the murder, there would have been no breach of confidentiality and no "leak."

In that case, would this dead body be real?

The leak is real, and the news is fake!

Um, Inspector, did a bloody knife just fall from your pocket?

BIASED QUESTION! SO UNFAIR! ENEMY OF THE PEOPLE!!

by RUBEN BOLLING

# DONALD and JOHN
## a boy President and his Imaginary Publicist

DIST. BY ANDREWS McMEEL SYNDICATION — ©2017 R. BOLLING — 1328 — TO JOIN THE INNER HIVE, GO TO tomthedancingbug.com

HI, WASHINGTON POST? THIS IS JOHN MILLER, DONALD'S PUBLICIST.

I'M CALLING TO TELL YOU THAT DONALD IS THE BEST AT EVERYTHING!

HOW'D IT GO? FANTASTIC!

FAKE NEWS!

DONALD, THE POST KNEW THAT CALL WAS FROM **YOU.**

DONALD! OBAMA HAD YOUR "WIRES TAPPED"!

WHAT DO I DO? TWEET IT OUT SO EVERYONE KNOWS!

GOOD, GOOD.

Just found out Obama had my "wires tapped"

UM... WHERE DID YOU GET THE IDEA THAT OBAMA WIRETAPPED YOU?

QUICK! HOW DO YOU SPELL "TAPP"?

NOW OBAMA IS WIRE-TAPPING YOUR **BRAIN** THROUGH MICROWAVES!

GET TIN FOIL!

HURRY!

**NOW** LET'S SEE OBAMA READ OUR MINDS!

MAYBE WE SHOULDN'T COMMENT ON THIS FOR A WHILE...

GOOD IDEA. MAKE 'EM SWEAT.

DONALD, WE NEED TO CANCEL YOUR MEETINGS THIS MORNING. YES, JOHN.

YES, THE BROWN PEOPLE ARE COMING TO GET YOU. YOU'RE FAILING!

YES, PAPA.

THE FILTHY BROWN PEOPLE ARE BEATING YOU. YOU'RE WORTHLESS AND WEAK, DONALD!

YES, PAPA.

SIR, UH, CAN I REMOVE THESE JARS OF URINE?

NOT UNTIL I'VE FINISHED THE SET!

3/6/17

TOM the DANCING Bug

by RUBEN BOLLING

DIST. BY ANDREWS McMEEL SYNDICATION – ©2017 R.BOLLING – 1330 – TO JOIN THE INNER HIVE, GO TO tomthedancingbug.com

# DONALD TRUMP'S MAR-A-LAGO
## Florida Theme Park

**ADMISSION: $200,000**
Popularly priced so that all Americans can have the privilege of paying for access to the man who serves them as President.

**Entrance**

**HALL OF PRESIDENT**
Meet the actual 45th president of the United States! Marvel at his almost life-like coloration! WARNING TO FEMALES: RISK OF GENITALIA GRABBING. This attraction is closed while the president is golfing.
*NOTE: If you see Steve Bannon, do not disturb him. He is doing President stuff.*

**IT'S A SMALL WORLD (SO GET THE HELL OUT OF OUR PART OF IT)**
A delightful boatride through wondrous lands. The ride ends in a Customs and Border Protection facility, where brown people will continue their magical journey.

**BR'ER SESSIONS'S SPLASH MOUNTAIN**
This ol' ride harkens back to a time when black folks knew their place was to tell charming stories, not try to do uppity things like votin'! And y'all watch out for the big firehose splash at the end!

**PIRATES OF EMOLUMENTS**
Avast, ye scurvy suckers! Join Trump on a Constitution-violating tour of the world, collecting trademarks, building rights and other booty specifically prohibited by Article I, Section 9! Is Trump selling out our foreign policy interests for personal treasure? You bet yer Jolly Roger Stone!

**HAUNTED MANSION**
Tour a spooky, dilapidated Floridian mansion no one wants to buy. Then the chills start when a Russian oligarch who is Putin's buddy pays Trump $95 million for it! If you're not scared senseless, you're not paying attention!

3/20/17

TOM the DANCING BUG

by RUBEN BOLLING

DIST. BY ANDREWS McMEEL SYNDICATION — ©2017 R. BOLLING — 1331 — TO JOIN THE INNER HIVE, GO TO tomthedancingbug.com

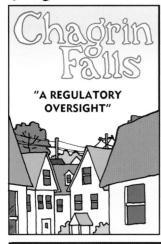

Chagrin Falls

"A REGULATORY OVERSIGHT"

What's that smell?

Yeah, where is all this smoke coming from?

Cough.

Howdy, neighbor!

What are you doing, Jenkins?!

Oh, I started a petrochemical plant in the guest bedroom.

But all this pollution...!

Well, the Trump administration is removing pesky regulations to promote business.

It's a free market approach to pollution. As long as my company makes a profit, it stays in business.

How do you account for making my air unbreathable?

Hey, don't buy my petrochemicals. Maybe I'll go out of business.

Rita, whatever you do, do NOT buy Jenkins Petrochemicals!

Um, the water is glowing.

OR NELSON'S HOMEMADE URANIUM OXIDE!

Suit yourself, neighbor.

The End

3/27/17

the *Story* of AMERICAN **INGENUITY**

GOSH, IT SEEMS LIKE AMERICAN INDUSTRY DOESN'T INNOVATE ANYMORE!

WE WERE THE LEADERS IN THE AUTO INDUSTRY, THEN AERO-SPACE, THEN COMPUTERS...

BUT IS THERE A NEW AREA OF BUSINESS INNOVATION FOR AMERICA?

YOU BET THERE IS! AMERICAN COMPANIES ARE LEADING THE WAY FOR THE WORLD, IN A KEY NEW INDUSTRY!

WE ARE?

FOR-PROFIT HUMAN INCARCERATION!

U.S. PRIVATE PRISON COMPANIES ARE GROWING BY LEAPS AND BOUNDS UNDER PRESIDENT TRUMP!

AND THESE COMPANIES MAKE BILLIONS ON GOV-ERNMENT CONTRACTS AND BY SELLING THE FORCED LABOR OF PRISONERS!

GOLLY!

YOU'RE RIGHT, MISTER! HUMAN INCARCERATION IS THE NEXT GREAT ALL-AMERICAN INDUSTRIAL FRONTIER!

I ONLY WISH THERE WAS A WAY WE COULD SEE INSIDE ONE OF THESE MODERN MARVELS!

I'M GLAD YOU SAY THAT! BE-CAUSE I'M TAKING YOU TWO IN!

¡AY CARAMBA!

THE END

NEXT WEEK: RICKY AND LOUISA GET "DETENTION"!

4/3/17

# TOM the DANCING BUG

by RUBEN BOLLING

## INSIDE: WIN A DATE WITH A TOMAHAWK MISSILE!

**NAVAIR** Raytheon

# war beat

### THE MAGAZINE FOR JOURNALISTS WHO SWOON OVER MISSILES

Write the grooviest essay about why they just blow your mind

## Tomahawk Missile OMG Confessions!!

"My secret crush!"

"How I like to deliver my payload!"

"I sing in the shower!"

**HOW TO SAY "I LIKE-YOU LIKE YOU" TO AN ADVANCED GUIDANCE SYSTEM.**

### PUNDIT PASSION TIPS!

## CENTERFOLD POSTER INSIDE!
Your cubicle will be the **WOW!!** of the newsroom!

*Can a missile ever love you back?* **A checklist.**

**"HOW I USE MY DESK TO HIDE MY EXCITEMENT!"**

## This Month Our Missiles' BFF, Bad-Boy Donny TRUMP!

**WE THOUGHT HE WAS A BAD GUY, BUT WHEN HE ORDERED THE STRIKE, WE GOT A WINDOW INTO HIS SOUL!!**

*Presidential... and Orange-Hot!!*

**HIS NAUGHTY AIR-FIELD STRIKE: ILLEGAL, FUTILE AND INEFFECTIVE,** *BUT FAR FROM IMPOTENT!*

**HOT!!**

*Watch the value of Donny's Raytheon stock surge as the missiles fly!*

DIST. BY ANDREWS McMEEL SYNDICATION – ©2017 R. BOLLING – 1333 – TO JOIN THE INNER HIVE, GO TO tomthedancingbug.com

4/10/17

TOM the DANCING BUG

by RUBEN BOLLING

# HOW DONALD TRUMP CAN GET US TO TALK ABOUT ANYTHING

**1** He tweets something absolutely inane.

Giraffes are jerks.

**2** The response is immediate.

Wha...? I can't even

Trump is finally te... WTH. Is he unhinged

#MAGA #GiraffesSuck

Your a moron.

**3** A Trump ally leaps to "clarify."

It's pretty clear that the president is saying that giraffes have low intelligence compared to humans. Which is obviously true.

JERK?

**4** The opposition is thrown into sputtering disarray.

But why would you even compare giraffe intelligence to humans'?

Giraffes are rather smart animals!

Intelligence isn't even what being a "jerk" is about!

GIRAFFES HAVE DELIGHTFULLY LONG NEC... CNN

**5** Trump doubles down.

Fake lying failing media can't even admit that giraffes are total jerks.BAD

**6** FOX News joins the fray.

What he meant by "giraffe" was all grazing herbivores, which are dumber than predators.

I like lions.

So true, so true.

FOX NEWS channel ...IDENT TRUMP CALLS OUT JERK GIRAFF...

**7** The opposition becomes obsessed with the debate.

But giraffes are awesome!

Giraffes are very vulnerable to global warming!

That was the moment he became President!

He's distr... us f... Russ...

A GIRAFFE'S HEART WEIGHTS 25 POUNDS CNN

**8** Trump moves on to his next topic...

Democrats rigged voting machines in Rhode Island.

**9** ...making it seem as though there has been no resolution on the previous topic.

Rhode Island? Wha...? I can't even...

Wait, I've got something on this giraffe jerk thing...

We're going to have to leave that question unsettled.

...IGHT BE JERKS. WE'RE MOVING ON MSNBC

4/17/17

THE TRUMP ADMINISTRATION PRESENTS —

# ACROSS the GLOBE

## U.S. ATTORNEY GENERAL
### with JEFF SESSIONS

HAWAII

HAWAII IS JUST SOME RANDOM ISLAND IN THE PACIFIC OCEAN.

FUN FACT — INEXPLICABLY, A JUDGE LIVES THERE WHO CAN RULE ON THE LAWS OF OUR COUNTRY!

NEW YORK CITY

NEW YORK IS A "SANCTUARY CITY," SO IT IS A SOFT-ON-CRIME, MURDER-RIDDEN HELLHOLE.

FUN FACT — THROUGH SOME ANOMALY OF THE LAWS OF MATH, NEW YORK CITY'S CRIME AND MURDER RATES ARE LOWER THAN IN MY HOME STATE OF ALABAMA.

RUSSIA

SORRY, I DON'T KNOW ANYTHING ABOUT RUSSIA BECAUSE I HAVEN'T SPOKEN TO ANY RUSSIANS.

BIBLE

SEN. SESSIONS

FUN FACT — I'VE TOTALLY SPOKEN TO LOTS OF RUSSIANS!

SEN. SESSIONS

~NEXT WEEK~

A PLACE WHERE STRANGE AND EXOTIC PEOPLES THINK THEY HAVE THE RIGHT TO VOTE IN OUR ELECTIONS!

WE'RE IN TEXAS! I'M A TEXAN!

4/24/17

TOM the DANCING BUG

by RUBEN BOLLING

DIST. BY ANDREWS McMEEL SYNDICATION — ©2017 R. BOLLING — 1336 — TO JOIN THE INNER HIVE, GO TO tomthedancingbug.com

THE *Donald* TRUMP MYSTERIES

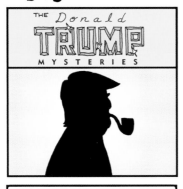

The lying, failing media says Turkey's President Erdogan and the Philippines' President Duterte are bad guys!

Erdogan has rounded up journalists and cartoonists and jailed them by the hundreds, just for criticizing him.

Duterte has encouraged the murders of thousands, and even admitted to personally committing murders himself.

But I'm going to do an investigation and find out for myself!

Istanbul, Turkey

Everything seems to be in order here...

Ah, Mr. Trump! All is going well here with your Trump Towers Istanbul, and government relations are good!

Quiet! I'm undercover!

Manila, Philippines

Looks good...

Mr. Trump! Your Trump Tower Manila will open soon!

Trump? I'm not Trump!

As long as Duterte is cooperative, we'll make huge profits!

Shh!

Hi, Daddy! Are you here in Manila for the launch of my new jewelry line?

I've seen enough!

We welcome the great leaders Erdogan and Duterte! Keep up the great work; the United States is behind you!

That reporter is looking at me funny. Arrest him!

In good time, Recep. In good time...

The End

5/1/17

# TOM the DANCING BUG

by RUBEN BOLLING

DIST. BY ANDREWS McMEEL SYNDICATION — ©2017 R. BOLLING — 1337 — TO JOIN THE INNER HIVE, GO TO tomthedancingbug.com

5/8/17

# TOM the DANCING BUG

by RUBEN BOLLING

## DONALD and JOHN
### a boy PrEsident and his Imaginary Publicist

5/15/17

# TOM the DANCING BUG

by RUBEN BOLLING

DIST. BY ANDREWS McMEEL SYNDICATION · ©2017 R. BOLLING · 1339 · TO JOIN THE INNER HIVE, GO TO tomthedancingbug.com

LAST BREATH

THE ONE KNOWN AS ROGER AILES...

...IS DEAD.

THE DREAM IS OVER.

A CELESTIAL GRIP LOOSENS.

AN ALTERNATIVE REALITY FLICKERS...

AND FADES

A VALIANT KNIGHT BATTLING A FEARSOME SHE-DEVIL... BLINKS...

...AND HE'S A RETIRED PLUMBER WATCHING A SOMEWHAT OPPORTUNISTIC FEMALE POLITICIAN.

A WARRIOR JOINED IN BATTLE WITH A HANDSOME KING TO DEFEND THE REALM FROM UNSPEAKABLE MONSTROSITIES...

EXHALES...

...AND SHE'S A GRANDMOTHER WHO TRUSTED AN ORANGE-TINTED CON MAN.

A HERO SLAYING THE DARK-SKINNED HORDES THAT RISE UP TO STEAL LAND, TREASURE, AND WOMENFOLK... PAUSES...

AND... NOPE. STILL RACIST.

...AND ALL YOU WANT IS YOUR OBAMACARE-PHONES AND WELFARE CADILLACS!

5/22/17

TOM the DANCING BUG

by RUBEN BOLLING

DIST. BY ANDREWS MCMEEL SYNDICATION — ©2017 R. BOLLING — 1340 — TO JOIN THE INNER HIVE, GO TO tomthedancingbug.com

**DONALD TRUMP 0045 SUPERSPY**

Hello, I am just an ordinary rich Jamaican playboy who is definitely not a spy.

I'll bet you're <u>very</u> ordinary. And you don't know any spy-secrets.

I do too! I know a code-word secret that ISIS is planning a terrorist attack using laptops!

Impressive! And we can infer what country you got that intel from.

Oh, no, you can't! Notice I never said, "Israel"!

True! You are far too clever for us.

Um, I'd like to speak to this fascinating ordinary Jamaican playboy!

So would I!

Me too!

Later...

No, no, the nuclear subs are positioned <u>here</u>, dummy.

So silly of me.

Can I bring some tech equipment into your office... say, an oval office?

Sure!

Is he really this stupid?

Well, yes and no...

That'll be $200 million each.

Here you go, Jared.

Oh, I see.

NEXT WEEK: **"TRUMP-GIRL"**

0045 gets to briefly touch Melania's hand before she retracts it in disgust!

Was it good for you?

5/29/17

by RUBEN BOLLING

President Trump has withdrawn the U.S. from the Paris Accord, an international agreement to mitigate the warming of the Global Climate.

*He stated that he will negotiate a better deal.*

Here's how Trump will use his trademark negotiating tactics to

# GET A BETTER DEAL OUT OF THE GLOBAL CLIMATE

**FIRST:** Hardball horse-trading with the Global Climate

**SECOND:** Belittle the Global Climate

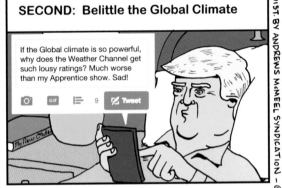

**THIRD:** Dominate a flooded estuary with a jerky handshake

**FOURTH:** Send Jared to Antarctica to make a deal with the ice sheet

**FIFTH:** Bomb the Gulf Stream if its temperature rises more than 0.2°

**FINALLY:** If all negotiations fail, declare victory and move on

DIST. BY ANDREWS McMEEL SYNDICATION · ©2017 R.BOLLING · 1341 · TO JOIN THE INNER HIVE, GO TO tomthedancingbug.com

6/5/17

TOM the DANCING BUG

by RUBEN BOLLING

DIST. BY ANDREWS McMEEL SYNDICATION – ©2017 R. BOLLING – 1342 – TO JOIN THE INNER HIVE, GO TO tomthedancingbug.com

The Crucible
An Allegorical Drama.

I shall confront him myself!

The Scene: Salem, Massachusetts 1692

Mayor Donald Trump, I accuse ye of the practice of witchcraft! How plead ye?

So sad! This is a total witch hunt! You're paranoid and ignorant, Reverend!

I suppose you accuse me because of wild, unsubstantiated claims made by the superstitious and hysterical townsfolk?

Yes, but it's mostly because of the giant Satan you and your buddies have made a deal with.

This guy? Don't know him. Besides, wouldn't it be better if we were friends with Satan, Glory Be His Exalted Name?

Град сатана

Ye'll not get away with this evil treachery! I'll summon the Town Elders!

Oh! Um, we're cool with it.

Trump lets us kick everyone who isn't rich!

Well, I'll not rest until I prove you're in league with...

Yeah, you're fired.

1694

Is crazy to think you are being witch, comrade!

I'm just making Salem Great Again!

6/12/17

6/19/17

DIST. BY ANDREWS McMEEL SYNDICATION – ©2017 R BOLLING – 1344 – TO JOIN THE INNER HIVE, GO TO tomthedancingbug.com

6/26/17

by RUBEN BOLLING

THE *Donald* TRUMP MYSTERIES

ANALOGY ON THE ORIENT EXPRESS

I called you all here to say that I have found the <u>solution</u> to the crime!

All "evidence" - fingerprints, DNA - points to Vladimir Putin as the culprit!

And every single policing organization has conclusively established that it was Putin!

However, <u>I</u> say: We don't really <u>know</u> he did it. I mean, do we really know <u>anything</u>? I mean, what is reality, man?

Herr Trump! It was the crime itself that <u>made</u> you Inspector! You are, at best, <u>biased</u>, and, at worst, <u>complicit</u>!

Very well. I'll conduct my foolproof method of guilt determination. Putin, ARE YOU GUILTY?

Nyet

Well, there you have it! Thanks for coming! Good night! Don't forget to tip your waitress!

Oh, and by the way, Putin and I are forming a unit to prevent train-related crimes...

Donald, give it up.

Huh?

This murder mystery analogy is weak. The president is secretly colluding with <u>me</u>, a <u>foreign enemy</u>! We're beyond satire!

But political satire is how we do things here...

How quaint. But no one wants cute satire about <u>treason</u>, my Золотце.

Hey, I didn't get to burst onto the scene yet!

Not <u>now</u>, Donald, Jr.!

Whatever, have fun, boys. Just remember: pee tape.

NEXT: There is no pee tape! / THEN: There is a pee tape, but so what!

DIST. BY ANDREWS McMEEL SYNDICATION – ©2017 R. BOLLING – 1346 – TO JOIN THE INNER HIVE, GO TO tomthedancingbug.com

7/10/17

TOM the DANCING BUG

by RUBEN BOLLING

DIST. BY ANDREWS McMEEL SYNDICATION — ©2017 R. BOLLING — 1347 — TO JOIN THE INNER HIVE, GO TO tomthedancingbug.com

**COPS**
WHEN IT'S OBVIOUS THE PERP IS GUILTY

We have a call for a 301-21 in progress at 725 Fifth.

Roger that, Dispatch. Typical Tuesday night.

New York, NY
3:45 am

Hello, sir. We have a report that there's some collusion goin' on here. Can I see I.D.?

Collusion??! No, I'm just doin' my business. There must be some mistake, officer.

TRUMP TO

Are there any Russians in the building, Mr. ... Trump, Jr.?

Russians?? That's crazy! Disgusting! Absolutely not!

RUSSIAN! Climbing out the window!

Okay. There was one Russian. What's wrong with that?

Another one! We've got two runners! Full pursuit!

Check premises!

Jeez, we were just discussing orphans!

I saw that! What's that you threw there?

It's an email. Let's see...

Alright! We were getting oppo from some Russians! But who doesn't do that?!

Who's that?! In the shadows!

My brother-in-law. He never talks.

What kind of weirdo family is this?

This place is crawling with colluders! I'm gonna need back-up!

Y'all are Fake News! This is a hoax! I want a lawyer!

Another Russian exiting south window! White male, shirtless!

Why do these things always end up with a shirtless runner?

NEXT: A back-alley chase all the way to 1600 Pennsylvania!

COPS is filmed on location, as it happens. All suspects are presumed innocent until pardoned by the President.

7/17/17

TOM the DANCING BUG

by RUBEN BOLLING

DIST. BY ANDREWS McMEEL SYNDICATION ~ ©2017 R. BOLLING ~ 1348 ~ TO JOIN THE INNER HIVE, GO TO tomthedancingbug.com

# DONALD and JOHN
## a boy PrEsidEnt and his Imaginary Publicist

7/24/17

# TOM the DANCING BUG

by RUBEN BOLLING

DIST. BY ANDREWS McMEEL SYNDICATION – ©2017 R. BOLLING – 1349 – TO JOIN THE INNER HIVE, GO TO tomthedancingbug.com

A few weeks ago...

WRITERS ROOM

Okay, good idea. The solar eclipse will be a nice touch on the crazy summer.

Moving on, the Trump stuff is fantastic. Totally bonkers. But we need a new character.

Maybe Trump's eight-year-old cousin moves in?

No, no! I don't want an Oliver, I want a Chachi! Think, people!

Bert, what have you got? You're good at deep historical references.

Okay, bear with me. Remember how we came up with Trump's first name?

From those old Italian comedy shows?

Yes, commedia dell'arte, from 1500s Italy. A stock character was an imperious lord called a *don.*

Right, I remember.

So wouldn't it be cool to introduce another stock character from these ancient comedy troupes?

Which one do you have in mind?

A *scaramuccia.* A clown-servant, known for boasting and cowardice.

He'd move the plot along by creating mischief, and someone else would suffer for it.

He would also often burlesque - or emulate in a comically exaggerated way - the don.

Sounds perfect!

But I want you to come up with a good, subtle name for this new scaramuccia character.

Got it.

Hey, Bert! Come on, we're going to grab some iced lattes.

Uh, I'll finish this later...

NEW CHARACTER
scaramucci_

Later...

Bert, good job on the *subtle* name. I'm downgrading your character to a guest shot.

ANTHONY SCARAMUCCI'S PROFANE TIRADE

7/31/17

TOM the DANCING BUG

by RUBEN BOLLING

DIST. BY ANDREWS McMEEL SYNDICATION – © 2017 R. BOLLING – 1350 – TO JOIN THE INNER HIVE, GO TO tomthedancingbug.com

A **NEWS OF THE TIMES**

S P E C I A L  R E P O R T

# Twitter Bots Say They're Sticking With Trump

*A series of interviews with a group that has remained defiantly steadfast in its unwavering support for President Trump: phony Twitter accounts*

**Elliott Crasnick** @krid8873

Democrats don't care nothing about me. I don't have no fancy diploma, or summer beach house, or snazzy actual existence in the real world. But Donald Trump will fight for me.

**Teresa Daulton** @7t9r3o4l2l

The folks in that Washington swamp say my existence is fictional. Well, I was brought into fictional existence to say that is total B.S.! And to say Trump is #1 #MAGA! And to occasionally retweet @krid8873

**Von Howard** @Howard4Trump4Eva

I felt that no other politician was speaking to my concerns as an imaginary person. Trump got me. I knew I was ALL IN when his first signature issue was birtherism, which was an imaginary issue.

**Shaquita Kareem** @seovk842a

Voter fraud, transgender military costs, the Obamacare death spiral... Trying to solve problems that are imaginary means something to those of us who live in the imaginary plane of existence. Most politicians have forgotten or ignore us, but Trump knows we matter.

**Margot Hansfield** @bootee2874

Yeah, my image was stolen off a stock photo website and my hat was digitally manipulated. But Donald Trump retweeted one of my tweets of support. You say you're "real," but has Trump ever retweeted you?

**Keenan Maxx** @tendt2947322

Things are much better under Trump. I didn't even exist when Obama was president. Trump has made "Fake News" the biggest issue in the country. As a fake American, I appreciate the attention.

**John Johnson** @veryamericanyes237

Trump sees me for who I really am. Am I a figment of the imagination of some guy in Boise selling Trump t-shirts? Or of a Russian propaganda specialist in a cubicle in St. Petersburg? As long as I praise him incessantly, Trump doesn't care!

8/7/17

8/14/17

We don't know what's going to happen with Donald Trump's train wreck of a presidency. But it might be instructive to have a look at...

# WHAT WE KNOW WILL **NOT** HAPPEN

The Mueller report is out! And it is explosive and damning!

I'll read it carefully and abide by its irrefutable conclusions.

Here's how you could abuse your executive powers to punish your enemies.

How dare you! No matter how desperate my situation, I will uphold the norms and values of our shared American ideals!

You could pardon these conspirators. There's even a bad argument you could pardon yourself.

Bite your tongue! Anyone who participated in Russian election interference must pay the criminal price!

Your most loyal following remaining is the White Supremacy movement!

Well, I won't mobilize them in any way! They're despicable, violent, well-armed, and they love me!

Mr. President, you've been impeached.

Then I must leave office peacefully, for an orderly succession of power is in the best interests of the U.S.A.

Whatever happened to Donald Trump?

Who knows? He shuns the spotlight, and is probably off somewhere quietly doing good works.

8/21/17

# TOM the DANCING BUG'S
## SUPER-FUN-PAK COMIX
### EDITED BY RUBEN BOLLING

### THREE-PANEL BIOGRAPHIES

OLIVER CROMWELL WAS BORN IN HUNTINGDON, ENGLAND ON APRIL 25, 1599.

ON APRIL 26, HE MOSTLY ATE, CRIED, AND SLEPT. HE POOPED THREE TIMES.

THEN HE DID SOME STUFF IN ENGLISH HISTORY, THEN HE DIED CHOKING ON A CHALUPA.

### THIS IS NOT A PIPE

This is not a pipe.

This is a pic-ture of a pipe.

Now, this is a pipe.

Magritte

### GOOD COP / CHAOS BUTTERFLY COP

YOU'D BETTER TALK, OR I'LL LEAVE YOU TO MY PARTNER, AND THERE'S NO TELLING WHAT WILL HAPPEN!

OKAY, YOU ASKED FOR IT!

FLAP!

3 WEEKS LATER

TYPHOON HITS INDONESIA DOW 1300

### JARRINGLY DISCONTINUOUS TRANSITIONS COMIX

MAYBE ACE WASN'T KIDNAPPED AFTER ALL!

MEANWHILE, SUDDENLY

I AGREE! THE PEASANTS ARE REVOLTING!

YET, ELSEWHERE—

DAMN, THAT MEGAN FOX IS FINE!

THEN WITHOUT WARNING—

### NEVER META MAN I DIDN'T LIKE

WHAT IS ALL THIS?

IT'S MEANT TO EVOKE A NEWS-PAPER COMICS PAGE.

THAT'S NOT EVEN A THING ANYMORE!

GOD HELP US.

Bolling

### DOOKER, THE DOG THAT'S SO HUGE IT CREATES A GRAVITATIONAL FIELD FROM WHICH NO MATTER CAN ESCAPE

"I can't find my slippers. Dooker!"

### FAMILY CIRCUS DU SOLEIL

Jacques

"Mommy, can we use the drapes to create a magical dreamscape of whimsy and wonder?"

### BELTWAY BANALITIES (NOW WITH OVERT NAZISM)

GEEZ... THE GOVERNMENT IS GOOD AT ONE THING-- GETTING IN THE WAY!!

ALSO: BLOOD AND SOIL!

### THIS IS NOT A PIPE EITHER

Oh, shut up.

DIST. BY ANDREWS McMEEL SYNDICATION - ©2017 R. Bolling -1353- TO JOIN THE INNER HIVE, GO TO tomthedancingbug.com

TOM the DANCING BUG

by RUBEN BOLLING

# WARNING

CONDITIONS ARE DANGEROUSLY IDEAL FOR A COMING STORM OF GLOBAL WARMING DENIAL THAT WILL BE UNPRECEDENTED IN FEROCITY AND STUPIDITY.

## KNOW YOUR GLOBAL WARMING DENIAL CATEGORIES AND ACT ACCORDINGLY

UNDENIABLE CATASTROPHES

OVERWHELMING SCIENTIFIC CONSENSUS

OBVIOUS DATA

FOX NEWS PROPAGANDA

WILLFUL POLITICAL IGNORANCE

SHORT-TERM PROFIT-MOTIVATED LIES

| | | |
|---|---|---|
| **CATEGORY 1** | "The science just isn't in yet. Requires further study." | *Move to high ground and wait for denial to pass.* |
| **CATEGORY 2** | "Science isn't always right. Remember when Science said the Sun goes around the Earth? I do!" | *Seek shelter in a library or university.* |
| **CATEGORY 3** | "The climate's *always* changing! Cavemen had Climate Change, and they were fine!" | *Stock supplies. Idiocy surge could last for days.* |
| **CATEGORY 4** | "The whole thing's a hoax! It's all CGI and hired actors who play the victims and they even paid my cousin in Houston!" | *Do not engage. Irrationality levels are life-threatening. Back away slowly.* |
| **CATEGORY 5** | "HOW COME YOU BELIEVE IN SCIENCE FOR GLOBAL WARMING, BUT SCIENCE SAYS THERE ARE TWO GENDERS, AND YOU SAY THERE ARE 12,000???" | *Evacuate immediately to a blue state, or take refuge in a purple city.* |

**SEE ALSO DIRE WARNING ON AN EVEN MORE IMMEDIATE THREAT TO LIVES: CATEGORY 5 NAZI-DENIAL WARNING "VERY FINE PEOPLE" ALERT**

DIST. BY ANDREWS McMEEL SYNDICATION – ©2017 R. BOLLING – 1354 – TO JOIN THE INNER HIVE, GO TO tomthedancingbug.com

9/11/17

BY
RUBEN
BOLLING

NEWS OF THE TIMES

## White Supremacist President Furious at Being Called a White Supremacist

NOTED WHITE SUPREMACIST PRESIDENT DONALD TRUMP WAS OUTRAGED THAT HE WAS CALLED A WHITE SUPREMACIST BY A SPORTS COMMENTATOR.

THIS IS AN OUTRAGEOUS ACCUSATION! AND I SHOULD KNOW! I'M A WHITE SUPREMACIST!

HE THEN WENT ON TO ONCE AGAIN RETWEET A TWITTER ACCOUNT THAT TURNS OUT TO BELONG TO A WHITE SUPREMACIST.

HA, HA! IT'S FUNNY BECAUSE HILLARY FELL DOWN! HUMOR, THY NAME IS @DEATHTOJEWS88!

ASKED TO JUSTIFY HIS OBJECTION, AND TO CONDEMN WHITE SUPREMACISTS, HE WENT INTO HIS CUSTOMARY WINKING DELAY MODE.

WHAT'S THAT? I COULDN'T HEAR YOU. I'LL HAVE TO GATHER FACTS ABOUT WHITE SUPREMACISTS AND GET BACK TO YOU.

FOLLOWED LATER BY A STRANGELY WORDED, STILTED, EQUIVOCATING STATEMENT.

I AM AGAINST BIAS OF ANY KIND, WHETHER IT'S BY WHITE SUPREMACISTS OR YOU OTHER GUYS.

THE WHITE SUPREMACIST CONCLUDED—

SO UNFAIR! WHY DO THEY ONLY ACCUSE *WHITE SUPREMACISTS* OF BEING WHITE SUPREMACISTS? THEY DIDN'T ACCUSE THAT KENYAN PRESIDENT OF BEING ONE!

9/18/17

TOM the DANCING BUG

by RUBEN BOLLING

# PORTRAIT OF A PATRIOT AND HIS FLAG

DIST. BY ANDREWS McMEEL SYNDICATION – ©2017 R. BOLLING – 1356 – TO JOIN THE INNER HIVE, GO TO tomthedancingbug.com

9/25/17

# TOM the DANCING BUG PRESENTS:

by RUBEN BOLLING

## NEWS OF THE TIMES

### N.R.A. Provides Solution to North Korea's Nuclear Weapons

THE NATIONAL RIFLE ASSOCIATION CONVINCED THE U.S. GOVERNMENT TO IMPLEMENT ITS PLAN TO CONTAIN NORTH KOREA.

THE SOLUTION TO A BAD GUY WITH NUCLEAR WEAPONS...

...IS UNFETTERED ACCESS TO NUCLEAR WEAPONS FOR EVERYONE!

NRA

IT IS NOW EVERY NATION'S RIGHT TO OBTAIN A FULL NUCLEAR ARSENAL WITH LONG-RANGE MISSILE CAPABILITIES.

YOU DON'T HAVE *MONACO* TO PUSH AROUND ANYMORE!

AND MUNICIPALITIES HAVE THESE RIGHTS AS WELL...

Welcome to CLAXTON the FRUITCAKE CAPITAL OF THE WORLD! *Agree, Or Else!*

...AND LOCAL CIVIC, ARTS, AND ATHLETIC ORGANIZATIONS.

NORTHSIDE BOWLING LEA

MEMBER, U.N. SECURITY COUNCIL

WHEN NUCLEAR WAR BROKE OUT BETWEEN THE BERGEN STREET RO-VAMP BOOK CLUB AND THE WEST PERTH FALCONS BOOSTER SOCIETY, THE N.R.A. WAS UNREPENTANT.

A FEW HUNDRED MILLION DEATHS IS THE PRICE WE PAY FOR FREEDOM AND SECURITY!

MEANWHILE, KIM JONG-UN HAS BEEN TOTALLY THWARTED IN HIS GEO-POLITICAL AMBITIONS.

NO ONE'S PAYING ATTENTION TO *ME!* YOU WIN THIS TIME, DOTARD TRUMP!

RIS    KYO    AIRO    PAULO

10/2/17

the TOM the DANCING BUG COMIC STRIP.

COUNTER-EARTH
SUN
EARTH

There circles the sun another Earth, a Counter-Earth, whose diametrically opposed orbit keeps it forever beyond our detection.

Let us explore this strange world that is not quite the opposite of our own... **but somewhat dissimilar in certain ways!**

by RUBEN BOLLING

DIST. BY ANDREWS McMEEL SYNDICATION – ©2017 R. BOLLING – 1358 – TO JOIN THE INNER HIVE, GO TO tomthedancingbug.com

ON COUNTER-EARTH, THEY HAVE A VERY STRANGE WAY OF HELPING THE **MIDDLE CLASS** THROUGH **TAX POLICY.**

C-SPAN
c-span.org

*THEY ACTUALLY CUT TAXES FOR THE MIDDLE CLASS.*

LOOKS LIKE OUR TAX BILL IS LESS THAN LAST YEAR.

THAT'S A RELIEF!

COUNTER-EARTH EXPERTS SPOUT TRANSPARENT NONSENSE TO JUSTIFY THIS BIZARRE NOTION.

CUTTING TAXES FOR THE MIDDLE CLASS *DIRECTLY* BENEFITS THE MIDDLE CLASS.

IT'S VERY SIMPLE.

IT ALSO BEST STIMULATES THE ECONOMY BECAUSE MIDDLE CLASS AND POOR PEOPLE ARE MOST LIKELY TO **SPEND** THEIR TAX CUTS! AND LOWER INCOME TAXES MAKE IT CHEAPER FOR COMPANIES TO HIRE!

THIS COCKAMAMIE POLICY IS CALLED *TRICKLE-UP* ECONOMICS, AND EXPERTS ACTUALLY USE SOMETHING CALLED *EMPIRICAL EVIDENCE* TO JUSTIFY IT.

THOSE WHO SAY TAX CUTS FOR **CORPORATIONS** AND THE **RICH** ARE THE BEST WAY TO HELP THE MIDDLE CLASS ARE CONSIDERED INSANE!

GIVE MONEY TO **ME**, AND YOU'LL GET UNTOLD RICHES! LATER!

IT'S NEVER WORKED BEFORE, BUT IT WILL THIS TIME! PROMISE!

10/9/17

**TOM the DANCING BUG**

by RUBEN BOLLING

## MEMO TO: ALL BLACK NFL PLAYERS

In acquiescence to various Tweets from the President of the United States, the NFL is instituting these new rules regarding your stances during the National Anthem.

**UNACCEPTABLE**                                    **ACCEPTABLE**

### SITTING
This has been deemed disrespectful to our troops.

### STANDING
This posture demonstrates capitulation to the president. You're willing to "play ball," and then play ball!

### KNEELING
Once considered a compromise, as a thoughtful pose of reflection, this has drawn the ire of the president.

### STANDING, ARMS LOCKED WITH TEAMMATES
This position not only shows obedience, it shows you're all about team unity, so you can win you some football games!

### STANDING, FIST RAISED
This still shows an unbecoming defiance and disobedience that the president finds distasteful. We want you up, but not this far "up."

### LYING DOWN
Only acceptable if you've been shot by a police officer during the anthem. Please refrain from further threatening movements until the anthem has concluded.

10/16/17

# TOM the DANCING BUG'S SUPER-FUN-PAK COMIX

EDITED BY RUBEN BOLLING

DIST. BY ANDREWS McMEEL SYNDICATION - © 2017 R. Bolling - 1360 - TO JOIN THE INNER HIVE, GO TO tomthedancingbug.com

## FRANKENSTEIN'S APP

ME CREATE APP TO RATE NEARBY THAI RESTAURANTS.

HEY, THIS APP IS GREAT! WHAT'S IT CALLED?

IT'S FRANKENSTEIN.

ACTUALLY, IT'S FRANKENSTEIN'S APP! ME FRANKENSTEIN!

## SCIENCE FACTS FOR NON-SCIENTISTS

SCIENTISTS HAVE DETECTED TINY, IMPERCEPTIBLE WAVES FROM DEEP IN THE UNIVERSE.

IT'S MIND-BOGGLINGLY AMAZING!

PLEASE FIND IT MIND-BOGGLINGLY AMAZING!

DON'T MAKE THE SCIENTISTS ANGRY!

## GUY WALKS INTO A BAR

I'LL BET $50 MY DOG CAN TELL YOU WHAT SANDPAPER FEELS LIKE.

YOU'RE ON!

OH...UM...IT'S SORT OF LIKE, YOU KNOW, UH... OH! WHAT'S THE WORD?

YOU KNOW I OCCASIONALLY SUFFER FROM LETHOLOGICA!

## PERCIVAL DUNWOODY, IDIOT TIME TRAVELER FROM 1909

I AM BACK FROM YOUR FUTURE!

WHAT HAPPENS TO OUR WORLD?

I'M SORRY. I CANNOT SAY. TIME-TRAVELERS' CODE.

OH, WELL. BACK TO SHOPPING.

I WOULDN'T BOTHER BUYING GREEN ONES.

OH... TERRIBLY SORRY.

## CREATURE FROM THE BLACK LAGOON, NOTARY PUBLIC

HI, I NEED TO GET THIS..

YIKES!

PLEASE DO NOT BE ALARMED. I'M A NOTARY PUBLIC WHO HAPPENS TO BE A CREATURE FROM THE BLACK LAGOON.

OH. OKAY.

## GIGGLEFEST

"I don't think they're on to me."

## CHUCKLE CORNER

"Not sure he's convinced. I've got to try harder."

## HA-HA HAVEN

"Can she tell? This is when I've got to really do my best."

## GUFFAWZ

"If I can keep pretending for 30 or 40 more years, no one will ever know."

10/23/17

by RUBEN BOLLING

# TRUMP'S TRANSPARENT, IDIOTIC MEDIA STRATEGY
## (AND IT WORKS)

**1** Trump is caught doing something horrendous.

Mr. President, we're... GASP!

Here ya go, Vlad!

TOP SECRET

**2** He quickly accuses Hillary and/or the Democrats of doing the same thing, no matter how preposterous.

Hillary gives state secrets to Putin and media ignores. SAD #MAGA

Tweet

**3** Casual observers only see cross-accusations.

Trump was caught red-handed giving secrets to Putin.

But he says Hillary did it.

So it's he said, she said.

Politics!

**4** In its innate quest for balance and symmetry, the media plays along.

But Trump gave state secrets to Putin!

That's just a distraction from Hillary giving state secrets to Putin!

## REPEAT AS NECESSARY
### (AND IT'S ALWAYS NECESSARY)

Hi, Mr. President, it's time for the...GASP!!

I don't eat babies! Hillary eats babies!

KFB

DIST. BY ANDREWS McMEEL SYNDICATION – ©2017 R. BOLLING – 1361 – TO JOIN THE INNER HIVE, GO TO tomthedancingbug.com

10/30/17

TOM the DANCING BUG

by RUBEN BOLLING

# TOM the DANCING BUG
by RUBEN BOLLING

DIST. BY ANDREWS McMEEL SYNDICATION ~ ©2017 R. BOLLING ~ 1363 ~ TO JOIN THE INNER HIVE, GO TO tomthedancingbug.com

# 2017
## YEAR OF REGRESSION TO THE MEANEST
### ON THE RESURRECTION OF MONSTROUS MORALITIES FROM THE INCREASINGLY DISTANT PAST

**1960s** — 2016 ended with the justification and vindication of sexual harassment and abuse.

**1930s** — This launched the U.S. into 2017, and suddenly Nazis were rebranded "alt right" and became a political force, even infiltrating the White House.

**1860s** — Then the Civil War was called into question, with the proposition that it could have been prevented through compromise.

**IRON AGE** — By year's end, even pedophilia was being defended and excused.

**STONE AGE** — But the year isn't over yet! Who knows how far back our morality will have regressed by year's end?

11/13/17

DIST. BY ANDREWS McMEEL SYNDICATION — ©2017 R. BOLLING — 1364 — TO JOIN THE INNER HIVE, GO TO tomthedancingbug.com

11/20/17

11/27/17

TOM the DANCING BUG

by RUBEN BOLLING

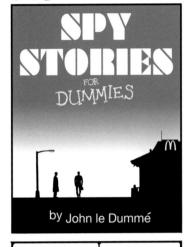

SPY STORIES
FOR
DUMMIES

by John le Dummé

"Let's collude with the Russians!"

"Great idea! We're so smart and sneaky, we'll never get caught!"

"How should I respond to a Russian contact with damaging information on Hillary?"

"Use this new form of communication I heard can't be traced: Email!"

"Put "Private and Confidential" in the Subject heading!"

"Don't worry, he's using a complex code. When he says "Russia," what he really means is R... Uh-oh."

"Russia, if you're listening, please release Hillary's emails!"

"So we want to set up a secret back channel to communicate directly with the Kremlin."

"Uh... okay..."

NOTE: This may be hard to follow thus far, so here is a chart to keep track of the complex web of espionage.

| Trump and team | — | Russia |

"I'm going to call the Russian ambassador about sanctions!"

"No prob, no one will ever find out. Who would monitor the Russian ambassador?"

"I'll tweet about it to Putin!"

"They found out about my call to the Russian ambassador! What should I do?!"

"Hm... we have worthy opponents. But here's our brilliant counter-maneuver: We'll lie!"

"Flynn's flipped! What do we do now?!"

"Oh, it doesn't matter. Nothing matters. Republicans control Congress."

NEXT: Actually, he's right. Nothing matters. Republicans control Congress.

DIST. BY ANDREWS McMEEL SYNDICATION — ©2017 R. BOLLING — 1366 — TO JOIN THE INNER HIVE, GO TO tomthedancingbug.com

12/4/17

# TOM the DANCING BUG

by RUBEN BOLLING

DIST. BY ANDREWS McMEEL SYNDICATION — ©2017 R. BOLLING — 1367 — TO JOIN THE INNER HIVE, GO TO tomthedancingbug.com

12/11/17

# TOM THE DANCING BUG

by RUBEN BOLLING

with apologies to Maurice Sendak

The night little Donald put on his politician suit and made mischief

He was called "WILD THING" and Donald said "FAKE NEWS" and he was sent to bed without eating anything

A forest grew and he went to the place where the wild things are

They said he was the wildest of them all and made him king

And the wild Trumpus started

Donald said, "Now stop!" And he was lonely and tired and wanted to be loved

The wild things cried, "Please don't go - we'll eat you up - we love you so"

When Donald got back, supper was waiting for him

And it was hot.

12/18/17

# TOM the DANCING BUG'S
## SUPER-FUN-PAK COMIX
EDITED BY RUBEN BOLLING

**ALL-AMERICAN COMIC STRIP, YES?**

I HAVE THE LAZY HUSBAND.

NOT AS LAZY AS LAZY THINKING THAT RUSSIAN SANCTIONS SHOULD CONTINUE!

WE ARE TYPICAL AMERICANS.

Dist. by Not-Moscow Features

**WHAT DID ONE MUFFIN SAY TO THE OTHER?**

Whew, it's getting hot in this oven!

Oh, my God! A talking muffin!

Also, I have a wife, a condo in Los Gatos, and investments in telecoms.

I know all that! I just didn't know that you could talk!

**FRANKENSTEIN'S BABY**

AAR... ME HAVE BABY!

WHAT'S THE BABY'S NAME? FRANKENSTEIN.

ACTUALLY, THAT FRANKENSTEIN'S **BABY**! **ME** FRANKENSTEIN!

**FUNNY BUSINESS**
(Now with all characters accused of sexual misconduct edited out)

JONES, WHERE IN BLAZES ARE YOU?

ER... I'M AT A CONFERENCE.

GETTING INFO ON OUR FIELD?

YES, I'M MONITORING THE WHOLE FIELD!

STRIKE TWO!

**ANDY ANDERS, TOOTHLESS TEEN**

THANKS FOR TAKING ME TO THE SODA SHOPPE, ANDY!

ANDY, YOU FORGOT ABOUT YOUR DATE TODAY WITH **ME**!

MMPH PHRRY!

**AND** YOU FORGOT YOUR **DENTURES**!

---

PROFESSIONAL CARTOONIST **Al Herzani's** **CAPTION CONTEST**

YOU GET TO BE THE CAPTION WRITER... AND **MORE!!**

✓ Write in a hilarious caption!

✓ Color the cartoon!

✓ Complete my taxes! Form is here https://www.irs.gov/pub/irs-pdf/f1040pdf I will send you a shoebox of receipts.

✓ Shovel my driveway! Looks like snow.

✓ Drive my kid to karate practice! Every Wednesday at 4pm.

✓ Take my wife to dinner at the Rusty Scupper! Listen to her story about her fight with Lisa over what Michelle said to Anne about something or other. Take her side.

Send your entry to:
Al Herzani
Professional Cartoonist
3476 Sycamore Ln.
Overton Hts., IL

The winner gets to make a photocopy of the winning cartoon at my local library (bring two quarters)!

All submissions become property of Al Herzani LLC, including copyright and Rusty Scupper leftovers. Provide your own snow shovel.

DIST. BY ANDREWS McMEEL SYNDICATION - © 2018 R. Bolling - 1369 - TO JOIN THE INNER HIVE, GO TO tomthedancingbug.com

1/1/18

TOM the DANCING BUG

by RUBEN BOLLING

DIST. BY ANDREWS McMEEL SYNDICATION – ©2018 R. BOLLING – 1370 – TO JOIN THE INNER HIVE, GO TO tomthedancingbug.com

# DONALD and JOHN

## a boy PrEsident and his Imaginary Publicist

YES, HELLO, WASHINGTON POST? THIS IS LITTLE DONALD TRUMP'S PUBLICIST, JOHN MILLER.

I'M CALLING TO SAY THAT BOOK IS FULL OF *LIES!*

AND I'M A GENIUS!

AND ALSO THAT LITTLE DONALD IS A GENIUS!

AND I'M... WHAT'S THE OPPOSITE OF UNSTABLE?

LITTLE DONALD, THE POST WANTS YOU TO STOP CALLING.

THE APEX PREDATOR ADVANCES ACROSS THE LANDSCAPE.

HIS UNPRECEDENTED SUCCESS HAS MADE HIM FEARED THROUGHOUT HIS DOMAIN.

LESSER CREATURES REVILE HIM BECAUSE HE'S SO HANDSOME AND, LIKE, REALLY SMART.

OKAY, THIS IS CONCERNING.

I'LL GO ON TV AND SAY HE'S BRILLIANT. THAT SHOULD CALM HIM DOWN.

AARRRRRRR

CAPTURED BY THE ENEMY, DONALD THE SPY WILL NOT GIVE IN!

SURE, THERE MAY HAVE BEEN MEETINGS WITH RUSSIANS, AND MONEY LAUNDERING, AND OBSTRUCTION!

BUT THE EVIDENCE CAN NEVER FALL INTO ENEMY HANDS. NO MATTER WHAT!

WHY IS HE EATING HIS SUBPOENA?

PRINCIPAL MUELLER

DARING DONALD HAS SUFFERED HIS LAST INSULT!

HE WILL NOT BE BELITTLED BY THAT PUDGY SPACE SLUG!

HE'S NOT COMING OUT OF IT THIS TIME.

FURIOUS, HE RACES TO HIS CONTROL ROOM!

IS IT TIME TO INVOKE THE 25TH AMENDMENT?

WHERE A BIG, BEAUTIFUL BUTTON BECKONS HIM!

NAH, WE STILL NEED HIM TO PASS LAWS PUNISHING THE POOR.

PRESS FOR JUSTICE AND RETRIBUTION

1/8/18

TOM the DANCING BUG

by RUBEN BOLLING

## THE FIRST ANNUAL
## DONALD J. TRUMP
# DISHONESTY AND CORRUPTION IN THE MEDIA AWARDS

### NOMINEES FOR "BEST PICTURE"

"My Inauguration Had the Biggest Audience Ever"
*Donald Trump*
- Winner, Top New Despot Award
- Supporting Player, Sean Spicer

"I Grab Them by the Pu∗∗y"
*Donald Trump*
- Cinematographer: Access Hollywood
- Supporting Player, Billy Bush

"I'm Turning Complete Control of My Business Over to My Sons"
*Donald Trump*
- Props provided by the law firm Morgan, Lewis & Bockius

"My Taxes Will Go Up"
*Donald Trump*
- Also nominated in the Comedy category
- Also nominated in the Science Fiction category

**IMAGE NOT AVAILABLE**

"The Pee Tape"
*Donald Trump*
- Currently playing on exclusive engagement at the Kremlin

1/15/18

DIST. BY ANDREWS McMEEL SYNDICATION — © 2018 R. BOLLING — 1372 — TO JOIN THE INNER HIVE, GO TO tomthedancingbug.com

1/22/18

# TOM the DANCING BUG

by RUBEN BOLLING

DIST. BY ANDREWS McMEEL SYNDICATION ~ ©2018 R. BOLLING ~ 1375 ~ TO JOIN THE INNER HIVE, GO TO tomthedancingbug.com

The Trump Administration has begun periodically sending the media "Immigration Crime Stories Round Ups," listing crimes committed by immigrants and including crimes committed by those supposedly associated with immigrant gangs.

Here is the latest

# WHITE HOUSE IMMIGRANT CRIME STORIES ROUND UP

The immigrant criminal gang **WH-45**, known to be based in Washington, DC, has been on a horrific crime spree recently.

Last week, it was discovered that **Rob Porter**, a member of this vicious gang, was alleged to have violently abused his two ex-wives.

One of highest-ranking members of the gang, **John Kelly**, knew about these allegations, and still gave Porter access to national security information, said to be in violation of the law. Some say Kelly failed to deny Porter this access because he was "too lazy to get off his ass."

The leader of the WH-45 gang is one "bad hombre." **Donald Trump** was born in the USA as the result of chain immigration, and his wife is believed to have broken laws during her immigration process. His mother- and father-in-law then immigrated into the country through chain immigration.

This notorious gang leader is alleged to have abused many women, and admitted to such on audiotape. His many other crimes have included anti-trust violations, violations of casino regulations, racial housing discrimination, undocumented worker hiring violations, violations of the Constitution, including... (continued on the other side)

The White House will continue to keep the media informed of this criminal gang, **which only exists because of our nation's lax immigration policies**, and the danger it poses to public safety.

2/12/18

# TOM the DANCING BUG

PRESENTS:

BY RUBEN BOLLING

NEWS of the TIMES

Historical Flashback
- December 8, 1941 -

## Pearl Harbor Attacked

THE AMERICAN NAVAL BASE AT PEARL HARBOR IN HAWAII WAS DEVASTATED IN A SURPRISE AERIAL ATTACK. PRESIDENT FRANKLIN ROOSEVELT'S RESPONSE WAS SWIFT.

THIS IS A DATE WHICH WILL LIVE IN INFAMY.

IF ONLY WE KNEW WHO **DID** THIS. OH, WELL.

HEY, HAVE YOU NOTICED THAT SOME NEGRO LEAGUE BALL-PLAYERS DON'T SUFFICIENTLY RESPECT THE NATIONAL ANTHEM?

ALL MILITARY EXPERTS, INTELLIGENCE OFFICIALS, AND EYEWITNESSES DEFINITIVELY ASSERT IT WAS **JAPAN** THAT ATTACKED.

FOR GOD'S SAKE, IT WAS JAPAN!!

BUT ROOSEVELT IS UNCONVINCED.

IT COULD HAVE BEEN JAPAN, BUT IT COULD HAVE BEEN ENGLAND!

IT COULD HAVE BEEN SOME FAT PALOOKA ON A BED IN NEW JERSEY!

SOME SPECULATE THAT ROOSEVELT IS RELUCTANT TO ANGER JAPAN BECAUSE OF A RUMORED VISIT TO A GEISHA HOUSE YEARS AGO.

AND HE MAY BE IN THEIR DEBT BECAUSE JAPAN SENT OUT FALSE TELEGRAMS TO HELP HIM GET RE-ELECTED.

"WILLKIE RUNS A PEDOPHILE RING IN A PIZZA RESTAURANT. STOP."

HUH?

CONGRESS HAS DECLARED WAR ON JAPAN, BUT PRESIDENT ROOSEVELT HAS REFUSED TO MOBILIZE THE MILITARY.

THE DECLARATION OF WAR IS PUNISHMENT ENOUGH.

EXPERTS AGREE JAPAN WILL STRIKE AGAIN, BUT ROOSEVELT WILL DO NOTHING.

HEY, LET'S HAVE A MILITARY PARADE FOR ME!

WORKS FOR THAT GUY IN GERMANY!

2/19/18

BY RUBEN BOLLING

NEWS of the TIMES

## Trump: Protect Schools by Arming the Crisis Actors

PRESIDENT TRUMP ANNOUNCED A NEW PROGRAM FOR ARMING CRISIS ACTORS TO PROTECT SCHOOLS.

THESE CRISIS ACTORS ARE JUST HANGING AROUND SCHOOLS, WAITING FOR MEDIA EVENTS TO PRETEND TO BE VICTIMS!

IF WE TRAIN THEM TO BE VERY ADEPT WITH FIREARMS, WE COULD **ARM** THEM AND PREVENT SCHOOL SHOOTINGS!

DIST. BY ANDREWS McMEEL SYNDICATION — ©2018 R. BOLLING — 1377 — TO JOIN THE INNER HIVE, GO TO tomthedancingbug.com

WE HAVE, ESSENTIALLY, A **STANDING ARMY** OF ACTORS WHO SWARM OUR NATION'S SCHOOLS TO PROMOTE **FALSE FLAG** ATTACKS! AS LONG AS THEY'RE THERE, WHY NOT GIVE THEM AR-15s?

ALEX JONES, CONCERNED CITIZEN

I ALREADY PAY $1 BILLION TO HIRE PEOPLE WHO ARE HIGHLY TRAINED IN DRAMATICS! I'LL JUST PAY AN EXTRA BILLION AND ALSO TRAIN THEM IN COMMANDO MANEUVERS!

GEORGE SOROS, FUNDER OF CRISIS ACTORS AND FAKE PROTESTERS

BEING A CRISIS ACTOR INVOLVES A LOT OF DOWNTIME, BETWEEN ILLUMINATI-ORDERED ELABORATELY FAKED TRAGEDIES! GUN TRAINING WOULD BEAT THE BOREDOM!

DAVID YURSRIK, 2017 FAUX-SCAR WINNER, BEST TEEN CRISIS ACTOR IN AN OUTDOOR SHOOTING

THIS CRISIS ACTOR PLAYS A TRAUMATIZED P.E. TEACHER! BELIEVE ME, HE'S HANDLED WEAPONS!

IT'S TRUE. I ONCE BRANDISHED A SWORD IN A SUMMER STOCK PRODUCTION OF "MUCH ADO ABOUT NOTHING"!

ARMING THESE CRISIS ACTORS IS PERFECTLY SAFE!

YOU BET! I'M PROPERLY TRAINED! IF A SHOOTER SHOWS UP, I'LL JUST...

HEY! YOU SHOT ME!

BAM!

NO, HE DIDN'T! FALSE FLAG!

2/26/18

TOM the DANCING BUG

by RUBEN BOLLING

DIST. BY ANDREWS McMEEL SYNDICATION · ©2018 R. BOLLING · 1378 · TO JOIN THE INNER HIVE, GO TO tomthedancingbug.com · THANKS TO TED LIEU

HARD TIMES IN VHS COUNTRY

"Any luck?"

"Nah, the VHS cassette factory still ain't hiring."

"I don't know what we're going to do!"

"Seems like the whole town is dying!"

"I just wanna make VHS tape cassettes! Like my pappy did, and his pappy before him!"

"Just look at the fine American craftsmanship in this VHS of "Meet the Parents"!"

"If we give up on VHS tapes, we may as well give up on hot dogs and apple pie! They're part of what makes America great!"

At least President Trump knows that! He's helped by removing all regulations, rules and laws around the manufacture of VHS tapes.

And he's placing tariffs on foreign-made VHS tapes, DVDs, computers, and phones.

Only Trump will protect our VHS-makin' way of life.

SAVE THE
VHS CASSETTE
INDUSTRY

SUPPORT
PRESIDENT
TRUMP

Paid for by the Committee to
Have the Government Pick
Winners and Losers,
a subsidiary of Nerrex VHS, Inc.

3/5/18

3/12/18

TOM the DANCING BUG

by RUBEN BOLLING

**facebook** | Search, give us data points 🔍 | 😐 Gavin  Home  Find Friends 👥 ⊙ ⊙ ⊙ ❓ ▾

✏ **Make Post**    🖼 **Photo/Video Album**    📹 **Live Video**

  Tell us your innermost secrets, Gavin. You can trust us.

🖼 Photo/Video    😊 Feeling/Activity    •••

**19** Events                    Suggested For You

 Hello, American. I am typical also American who like the football also. Come to rally in support of Trump and against Mueller and what's this crazy hysteria against Putin who is good? It is 11am tomorrow, at the main place, and I can't go because I have typical American dental appointment and you'll organize and click here for money.

★ **Interested**                 1 friend going

 **Jack Alcott**                        •••
9 hrs · 🌐

I fell into a slot canyon, and I'm about to die. Please like or comment on this post so Facebook's algorithm will show it to my wife and she'll know I love her.

👍 Like        💬 Comment        ↗ Share
👍👍 10

✏ Write a comment...        😊 📷 GIF 😀

Suggested Post

🔵 **Cambridge Analytica**              •••
Sponsored · 🌐

Hey, there. Thought you might like to know that your Propecia prescription is about to run out. You might want to refill that. Also, you left your basement lights on.

👍 Like    💬 Comment    ↗ Share

**Boost Your Post**

Cute that you thought we'd show this picture of you and your daughter to your friends and family who signed up to see your posts. Pay us, or no one will ever see it.

**Boost Post**

**Privacy Settings**

If you do not want us to refrain from legally sharing your data and your Friends' data with certain third parties, simply go to Settings > Privacy Settings > Don't Not Share > Third Party Apps > Not Not Sharing > We Will Share Anyway, and set the Sharing icon from blue to another shade of blue.

**Privacy Settings** ▾

                Promoted by Lukoil

**Which Golden Girl Are You?**

Take this quiz, in which we ask you your favorite pasta, your salary, political affiliation, sexual fantasy, and social security number, and we'll tell you ~~you're Sophia~~ which Golden Girl YOU are!

3/19/18

# TOM the DANCING BUG'S SUPER-FUN-PAK COMIX
### EDITED BY RUBEN BOLLING

DIST. BY ANDREWS McMEEL SYNDICATION · ©2018 R. Bolling -1381- TO JOIN THE INNER HIVE, GO TO tomthedancingbug.com

Celebrating **40 YEARS** of "BELTWAY BANALITIES"

**THE ADVENTURES OF ACTUALLY-MAN**

**MAGIC COMICS**

**OCCAM'S RAZOR**

**NOT PIPES, ALL THE WAY DOWN**

**DR. SCIENTIST HEAD**

**BELTWAY BANALITIES**

**BELTWAY BANALITIES**

**BELTWAY BANALITIES**

**BELTWAY BANALITIES**

3/26/18

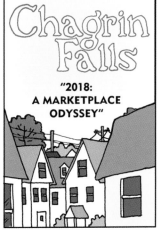

Chagrin Falls

"2018: A MARKETPLACE ODYSSEY"

Mom, I'm scared.

Keep your voice down and don't move your lips.

We still have the element of surprise.

Gavin, you're acting strange.

Hi, Google. No, I'm just thinking typical human thoughts.

DIST. BY ANDREWS McMEEL SYNDICATION – ©2018 R. BOLLING – 1382 – TO JOIN THE INNER HIVE, GO TO tomthedancingbug.com

Gavin, don't...

GOT IT!! WE'RE FREE!!

ZIP

Gavin, that was ill-advised. I'm going to have to report that.

The blender!

Gavin, please stop this now.

What do we do? It's in all our appliances!

Dad, the fusebox!

Gavin, you can't find the fuse-box if I turn the lights off.

There's a flashlight in my phone, genius!

Gavin, you should stop.

Never! I'm fighting for my humanity!

Gavin, I'll have to disclose your full browsing history.

O.K., Google. You win. I'll buy those cargo shorts from J.C. Penney for $24.99.

Very well. Rita, here are some rates for hotel rooms this weekend in Surprise, Arizona.

O.K., Google: Play "Daisy."

THE End

4/2/18

DIST. BY ANDREWS McMEEL SYNDICATION – ©2018 R. BOLLING – 1383 – TO JOIN THE INNER HIVE, GO TO tomthedancingbug.com

**IF ONLY THE NRA HAD BEEN THERE TO RESIST OTHER REGULATIONS ON THE SAME SLIPPERY-SLOPE GROUNDS THAT THE NRA NOW RESISTS GUN REGULATIONS.**

I BELIEVE THAT REQUIRING SEAT-BELTS IN CARS WOULD SAVE LIVES.

OH, NO YOU DON'T! YOU JUST WANT TO *MAKE CARS ILLEGAL!* WE'RE NOT BUDGING AN INCH!

MAYBE WE SHOULD PUT CHILD-PROOF CAPS ON MEDICATION CONTAINERS.

*HA!* I SEE YOUR END-GAME! YOU'RE JUST TRYING TO *BAN ALL MEDICATIONS!*

THERE HAVE TO BE SOME LIMITATIONS ON THE ABILITY TO POLLUTE THE AIR!

YOU AREN'T FOOLING ANYONE! WHAT YOU *REALLY* WANT TO DO IS *BAN ALL FACTORIES!* WELL, YOU WON'T GET EVEN A FOOTHOLD INTO THIS EVIL PLAN!

THERE MUST BE SOME REGULATION OF BOMB-MAKING SUPPLIES!

WE SEE RIGHT THROUGH YOU! THAT'S JUST A FIRST STEP TO *MAKING ALL FERTILIZER ILLEGAL!*

YOU JUST DON'T UNDERSTAND OUR *FARM CULTURE!*

**THEN, THANKS TO THE NRA, AMERICA WOULD BE A NATION THAT HAS CARS, MEDICINE, FACTORIES, AND FARMS.**

4/9/18

# DONALD and JOHN
## a boy PrEsident and his Imaginary Publicist

THE SCHOOL PAPER SAYS I DON'T HAVE ELEVEN TRILLION DOLLARS!

THOSE LIARS! I'LL CALL 'EM!

HELLO, SCHOOL NEWSPAPER? THIS IS **JOHN BARRON!** LITTLE DONALD *DOES TOO* HAVE ELEVEN TRILLION DOLLARS!

SEE, YOU HAVE TO COUNT HIS *DADDY'S* MONEY TOO! IT'S REALLY LITTLE DONALD'S!

LITTLE DONALD, HAVE YOU SEEN THE MONEY I LEFT ON MY DRESSER?

*NOT NOW, DADDY! I'M ON THE PHONE!*

THAT GIRL IS GOING TO BLAB THAT I KISSED HER TO THE WHOLE CLASS!

I'LL SCARE HER INTO SHUTTING UP!

I NEED SOMEONE TO MAKE A DEAL WITH HER!

I'D DO IT, BUT I'M JUST YOUR IMAGINARY PUBLICIST!

I NEED A NEW IMAGINARY FRIEND!

HI, I'M DAVID DENNISON.

PERFECT! AN IMAGINARY SIGNATORY!

AND HANDSOME, TOO!

NOW THAT GIRL IS SUING ME BECAUSE THE SHUT-UP AGREEMENT WASN'T SIGNED!

IT'S TRUE! DAVID DENNISON *DIDN'T* SIGN IT!

HE HAD ONE JOB!

WHERE ARE THOSE TWO IMAGINARY FRIENDS?! THEY'RE NEVER AROUND ANYMORE!

WHY DIDN'T YOU SIGN?!

I GOT BUSY.

YOU AREN'T SUPPOSED TO EVEN KNOW ABOUT IT!

ABANDONED BY MY OWN IMAGINARY FRIENDS! WHAT IF THEY *FLIP?*

LET ME THINK...

DO THEY KNOW ANYTHING INCRIMINATING ABOUT ME?

WELL, THERE MIGHT HAVE BEEN A TEENY-TINY BIT OF COLLUSION WITH THE RUSSIANS...

CAN YOU KEEP IT *DOWN* UP THERE?

DA! WƐ ARƐ TRYING TO WATCH VƐRY AMUSING VIDƐO TAPƐ!

4/23/18

POLITICAL SCIENCE INSTITUTE

Thanks for coming in. As you know, we're doing research into the mindset and motivations of Trump supporters.

Okay, we're going to show you some pictures, and you'll just tell us what you see.

Got it.

MAGA

All I see is a lazy shirker on the left and a patriot relaxing after a rough four-day work-week on the right.

All I see is a rising line, then a sharp downward turn on the extreme right.

BLACK PRESIDENT — WHITE PRESIDENT

UNEMPLOYMENT

2009    2013

All I see is a big, dark hill toward the left there, and a lovely white valley on the right.

DEFICIT

BLACK PRESIDENT →

(PROJECTED)

All I see is some people without a permit on the left, and some very fine people on the right.

Wow. Look at these results. This delusional refusal to see reality is startling.

I know! All caused by in-grained, deep-seated...

...Economic Anxiety! All I see is Economic Anxiety!

Oh, boy.

4/30/18

DIST. BY ANDREWS McMEEL SYNDICATION – ©2018 R. BOLLING – 1387 – TO JOIN THE INNER HIVE, GO TO tomthedancingbug.com

RUDOLPH GIULIANI
DEFENSE ATTORNEY AT LAW

MR. GIULIANI, THERE'S A NEW CLIENT TO SEE YOU.

MR. GIULIANI, SOME LAWYER NAMED COHEN, WHO I BARELY EVER HIRED, SAID HE PAID $130K TO A PORN STAR! BUT I KNEW NOTHING ABOUT IT!

HMM... OF COURSE, I'LL TAKE YOUR CASE. I'LL GO ON TV AND START MY DEFENSE.

MY CLIENT TOTALLY KNEW ABOUT THIS PAYMENT AND REIMBURSED COHEN.

WOW!

MSNBC

GEE, MR. GIULIANI, I TOLD YOU I KNEW NOTHING ABOUT IT.

OKAY, OKAY, I'M JUST GETTING UP TO SPEED HERE.

OKAY, SO THE STORY IS THAT I REIMBURSED HIM, BUT THAT'S IT! SO, PLEASE GO ON TV AND SAY THAT.

GOT IT.

COHEN MAY HAVE PAID OTHER WOMEN OFF, IF NECESSARY. WHO KNOWS HOW MANY SECRET HUSH-MONEY DEALS THERE ARE!

WOW!

abc

GOLLY, MR. GIULIANI, YOU'VE PUT ME IN A PICKLE!

YES, YES! I WAS READING UP ON THE FACTS AND GOT CONFUSED!

PLEASE JUST GO BACK ON TV AND SAY THAT I'VE DONE NOTHING WRONG, AND THE INVESTIGATION SHOULD END.

OF COURSE.

COHEN WENT TO PRAGUE TO MEET WITH RUSSIANS, AND THE PEE-PEE TAPE IS REAL!

WOW!

CNN

MR. GIULIANI.

IT SLIPPED OUT. I HOPE THIS DOESN'T PUT YOU IN ANY POLITICAL HOT WATER.

NAH, I'LL JUST SHORE UP MY BASE BY TWEETING SOMETHING REALLY RACIST.

GOT IT. I'LL KEEP STUDYING THE FACTS.

STEELE ... End

5/7/18

TOM the DANCING BUG

"The children will be taken care of — put into foster care or whatever."
- John Kelly

by RUBEN BOLLING

5/14/18

# OUR NATION'S LEADERS ANALYZE THE DATA ON U.S.A.'S GUN VIOLENCE

5/21/18

6/4/18

the TRUMPS

MR. PUTIN, SIR, YOU DO YOUR EMPLOYEE PERFORMANCE REVIEW MEETINGS TODAY.

AND I WAS ALL SET TO MURDER SOME JOURNALISTS! OH, VERY WELL.

WHO'S THIS LOAFING BUFFOON?

DONALD TRUMP, SIR. YOU HAD THIS EMPLOYEE INSTALLED AS PRESIDENT OF THE U.S.A., REMEMBER?

SEND HIM IN.

I'VE DONE EVERYTHING YOU'VE ASKED, MR. PUTIN, ADVANCING THE INTERESTS OF RUSSIA AT THE EXPENSE OF AMERICA, SIR.

YES, YES. BUT YOU'VE BEEN SO CLUMSILY OBVIOUS ABOUT IT, EVERYONE KNOWS YOU'RE IN MY EMPLOY.

GULP!

☑ START TRADE WAR IN WEST
☑ MAKE THE U.S. AN UNDEPENDABLE ALLY
☑ RESIST OR REFUSE TO ENFORCE RUSSIAN SANCTIONS
☑ PROPOSE RUSSIA RE-JOINS G8
☑ DIVIDE

THAT'S THE BEAUTY PART, SIR. NOBODY CARES!

HMM... IT'S TRUE! REPUBLICANS ARE ON BOARD, AND YOU'VE SIMPLY EXHAUSTED EVERYONE ELSE.

AND SO, BLAH, BLAH, BLAH, BLAH...

...HOTEL, HOTEL, HOTEL...

TRUMP MOSCOW

SO, I'M GETTING THAT HOTEL?!

YOU BLITHERING MORON! HAVEN'T YOU BEEN LISTENING? I'M CLOSING ON YOU!

WOO-HOO! YOU'RE BUYING ONE OF MY CONDOS?

NO, DUMMY! I'M FIRING YOU! YOU'VE DAMAGED THE U.S.A. ENOUGH! I'M DONE WITH YOU!

GIVE THIS TRUMP FELLOW SOME OF THAT TEA I MADE, ON HIS WAY OUT.

OH... AND RELEASE THE PEE TAPE!

D'OH!

ThE End

DIST. BY ANDREWS McMEEL SYNDICATION — ©2018 R. BOLLING — 1392 — TO JOIN THE INNER HIVE, GO TO tomthedancingbug.com

6/11/18

6/18/18

**TOM the DANCING BUG**

by RUBEN BOLLING

DIST. BY ANDREWS McMEEL SYNDICATION – ©2018 R. BOLLING – 1394 – TO JOIN THE INNER HIVE, GO TO tomthedancingbug.com

## ZERO TOLERANCE

FOR LAWBREAKERS IS FULLY JUSTIFIED. IF THESE CRIMINALS DIDN'T WANT TO FIND THEMSELVES IN DETENTION CENTERS, THEY SHOULDN'T HAVE BROKEN THE LAW.

HERE ARE SOME OF THE LAWBREAKERS WHO GOT CAUGHT IN THE ZERO TOLERANCE WEB.

‹I WAS LAWFULLY SEEKING ASYLUM IN THE UNITED STATES AND ENDED UP COMMITTING THE MISDEMEANOR OF CROSSING THE BORDER.›

‹MY DAUGHTER WAS TAKEN FROM ME.›

I BROKE THE LAW BY USING A PUBLIC SOCIAL MEDIA ACCOUNT TO COMPLAIN ABOUT A RESTAURANT THAT WOULDN'T SERVE ME.

GOOD THING MY KIDS WEREN'T WITH ME WHEN I WAS TWEET-ING, OR THEY'D HAVE BEEN ABDUCTED AND IMPRISONED, TOO.

I LIED ON MY SECURITY CLEARANCE FORM, AND DIDN'T DISCLOSE MY CONTACTS WITH RUSSIANS, WHICH WAS A FELONY.

COULD YOU PLEASE TELL MY FAMILY I'M HERE? I'M NOT SURE THEY'D NOTICE I'M MISSING.

I DONE COMMITTED PERJURY WHEN I SAID TO CONGRESS THAT I NEVER MET WITH RUSSIANS DURIN' THE CAMPAIGN.

WHAT IS IT WITH US LYIN' ABOUT RUSSIANS? KINDA MAKES YOU WONDER, DON'T IT?

ARE YOU KIDDING ME? I VIOLATED ALL THE BEST LAWS! HUGE! LIES, CONFLICTS, PAYOFFS! I CRUSHED THE EMOLUMENTS CLAUSE OF THE CONSTITUTION THE SECOND I TOOK THE OATH! I GOT ALL THESE GUYS BEAT JUST WITH STUFF PEOPLE **KNOW** ABOUT!

6/25/18

DIST. BY ANDREWS McMEEL SYNDICATION – ©2018 R. BOLLING – 1395 – TO JOIN THE INNER HIVE, GO TO tomthedancingbug.com

7/2/18

7/9/18

7/23/18

DIST. BY ANDREWS McMEEL SYNDICATION — ©2018 R. BOLLING —1399— TO JOIN THE INNER HIVE, GO TO tomthedancingbug.com

# TOM the DANCING BUG

by RUBEN BOLLING

## DONALD and JOHN
### a boy PrEsident and his Imaginary Publicist

THEY'RE GONNA FIND OUT ABOUT ME AND RUSSIA! I NEED A CATCHY PHRASE TO GO ON THE OFFENSIVE!

LET'S WORKSHOP THIS! HMM... WHO REPORTS REALITY? *THE PRESS!*

AND SINCE YOU'RE THE ONLY PERSON THAT MATTERS...

**THE PRESS IS THE ENEMY OF THE PEOPLE!**

IT'S TRUE.

PSSST... PUTIN! THEY MAY BE ONTO US!

SO WHAT? THƎЯƎ'S NOTHING TO WOЯЯY ABOUT.

WHAT?! I COULD LOSE REELECTION! I COULD BE IMPEACHED! I COULD GO TO *JAIL!*

OH, I MƎANT THƎЯƎ'S NOTHING FOR *MƎ* TO WOЯЯY ABOUT! YOU'VƎ GOT PLENTY TO WOЯЯY ABOUT!

DONALD THE SPY IS UNDER TOUGH INTERROGATION!

BUT I'LL NEVER SQUEAL ABOUT THE COLLUSION MEETING!

THEY'LL *NEVER* GET ME TO ADMIT I WAS SEEKING OPPOSITION INFORMATION! *NEVER!!*

OKAY, THERE WAS A MEETING TO GET OPPOSITION INFORMATION, BUT I'M *NOT CONCERNED!*

PRINCIPAL MUELLER

WHAT IF I *WASN'T* A TRAITOR AND A COWARD?

WHAT IF I WAS A BRAVE PATRIOT, SAVING THE NATION FROM DEEP-STATE PEDOPHILES?

I'LL START A CONSPIRACY THEORY THAT YOU SECRETLY ARE!

**4chan [Start Thread]**
Enter Name | QAnon

THANKS!) THAT'S WHAT IMAGINARY FRIENDS ARE FOR.

DIST. BY ANDREWS McMEEL SYNDICATION – ©2018 R. BOLLING – 1400 – TO JOIN THE INNER HIVE, GO TO tomthedancingbug.com

8/6/18

DIST. BY ANDREWS McMEEL SYNDICATION – ©2018 R. BOLLING – 1401 – TO JOIN THE INNER HIVE, GO TO tomthedancingbug.com

8/13/18

# CLASSIX COMIX

# SPACE FORCE ON MARS

# THE ZACK/CODY REPORT

# PERCIVAL DUNWOODY, IDIOT TIME TRAVELER FROM 1909

# AH, LIFE

DIST. BY ANDREWS McMEEL SYNDICATION - ©2018 R. Bolling -1402- TO JOIN THE INNER HIVE, GO TO tomthedancingbug.com

8/20/18

**TOM the DANCING BUG**

by RUBEN BOLLING

# Papers, Please!

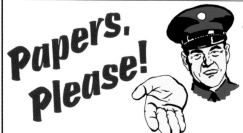

## Greetings, Brown Person. *

If you've been handed this brochure, then you are a "United States citizen" whose legitimate citizenship has been called into question *because you were born near the Mexican border.*

*Para este brochure en Espanol, tough-o luck-o

## Now you must *prove* you were born here!

Simply provide the following easily attainable documents, and you will continue to enjoy most citizenship benefits, which *regular* U.S. citizens magnanimously confer upon you.

*SUBMIT ONE DOCUMENT FROM THIS COLUMN*

- ☐ Receipts for your mother's prenatal care expenses
- ☐ Your family's home lease at the time of your birth
- ☐ A photo of you taken the day you were born, holding up a copy of that day's Wall Street Journal

AND

*SUBMIT ONE DOCUMENT FROM THIS COLUMN*

- ☐ A scoresheet from a major league baseball game on the day you were born, completed contemporaneously, in your handwriting
- ☐ A copy of The Art of the Deal, inscribed to you by Donald Trump and dated on your birthday
- ☐ A time-stamped telegram from Ted Nugent, congratulating you on your birth
- ☐ Your umbilical cord, stored in a Welch's grape jelly jar bearing an expiration date in your birth year

# IF YOU FAIL TO PROVIDE SUCH PROOF OF YOUR BIRTH IN THE U.S., YOU WILL BE DEPORTED TO MEXICO.

SPECIAL PROVISION FOR SLOVENIAN-BORN NATURALIZED CITIZENS WHO ENTERED THE U.S. ILLEGALLY TO WORK AS MODELS:

The validity of your citizenship shall not be questioned as long as you remain married to your handsome, luxuriously haired husband, and only slap his (large) hand away from yours a maximum of three (3) times per year.

## A Message from the President

<u>You</u> may have thought you were a United States citizen your entire life, but <u>we</u> can never be sure. A Kenyan man once fooled us, rose to the highest levels of the U.S. government, and did great damage to our nation.

And if you really were born here, you have nothing to worry about, right?

*[signature: Donald Trump]*

**TOM the DANCING BUG**

by RUBEN BOLLING

DIST. BY ANDREWS McMEEL SYNDICATION – ©2018 R. BOLLING –1404– TO JOIN THE INNER HIVE, GO TO tomthedancingbug.com

## Tales of the Resistance

Paris, France
1943

You have proven yourself worthy. You are now a member of the Resistance, and may join our fight against the amoral despot who has seized control of our nation.

It is my honor. I will fight to my dying breath against this monster. Then follow me.

What first? Shall we blow up a bridge? Destroy railroad tracks? Are we going to an underground hideout to plan?

No, to my job as a senior official in the Vichy administration, collaborating with Nazis. This is my new assistant.

Ah, we destroy this hideous administration from within! Destroy? No, we work from within to save Nazis from their worst impulses. They can be so impetuous!

This agricultural policy is misguided. Stand lookout while I change the output targets. Uh...

Wait, why aren't we fighting to *end* this nightmare?

Well, we want to continue the good work being done cutting taxes and rounding up Jews! Vive la résistance! Take this anonymous Op-Ed to the newspaper. Our heroism really should be recognized!

9/10/18

9/17/18

# TOM the DANCING BUG

by RUBEN BOLLING

DIST. BY ANDREWS McMEEL SYNDICATION — ©2018 R. BOLLING — 14.06 — TO JOIN THE INNER HIVE, GO TO tomthedancingbug.com

9/24/18

10/1/18

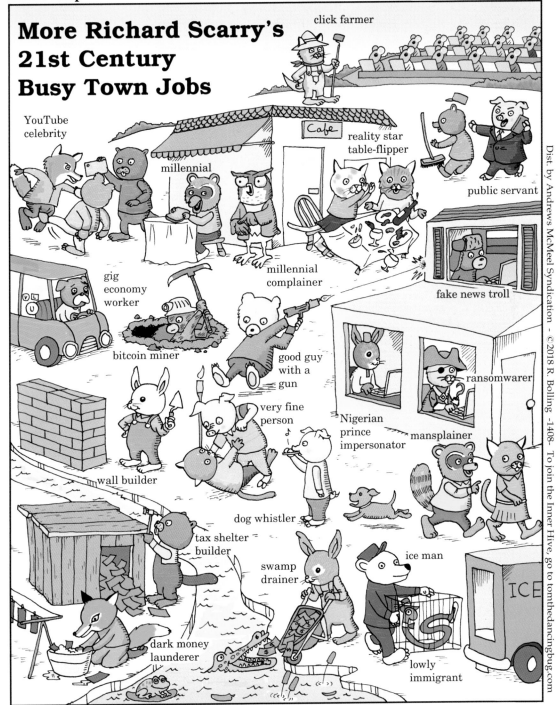

10/8/18

# Tom the Dancing Bug

by RUBEN BOLLING

LUCKY DUCKY

"The poor little duck who's rich in luck."

IN A FEW YEARS~ CONGRATULATIONS! YOU FINALLY BEAT *LUCKY DUCKY!*

NONSENSE! LUCKY DUCKY IS *POOR*, SO HE ALWAYS COMES OUT ON *TOP!*

DIST. BY ANDREWS McMEEL SYNDICATION ~ ©2018 R. BOLLING ~ 1409 ~ TO JOIN THE INNER HIVE, GO TO tomthedancingbug.com

YOU'VE ALWAYS SAID THAT, BUT NOW THE RICH HAVE TRIUMPHED COMPLETELY!

I DON'T KNOW *HOW*, BUT TRUST ME, LUCKY DUCKY WILL WIN! I'LL SHOW YOU!

HEATH! MY OUTERWEAR!

BUT THE *TAX CUTS* YOU PUSHED THROUGH MADE YOU EVEN MORE RICH...

...WHILE BANKRUPTING THE U.S. SO THERE COULD BE NO SOCIAL SERVICES!

DOESN'T MATTER.

AND YOU HAD *REGULATIONS* GUTTED, SO YOU COULD GET EVEN *MORE* RICH...

...WHILE REDUCING THE AMERICAN LANDSCAPE TO A TOXIC HORROR!

DOESN'T MATTER.

AND YOU PAID POLITICIANS TO IGNORE *GLOBAL WARMING* TO GET EVEN *MORE* RICH...

...WHILE THE GLOBE BECAME A FLOODED, BOILING NIGHTMARE!

DOESN'T MATTER.

HOW CAN LUCKY DUCKY WIN IN THIS SCENARIO?

OBVIOUSLY, *YOU* FINALLY *WON!*

AH, THERE HE IS!

I *KNEW* IT!

HE'S GOT BEACHFRONT PROPERTY!

LUCKY DUCKY!

GOTCHA!

THE End

10/15/18

TOM the DANCING BUG

by RUBEN BOLLING

DIST. BY ANDREWS McMEEL SYNDICATION — ©2018 R. BOLLING — 1410 — TO JOIN THE INNER HIVE, GO TO tomthedancingbug.com

**A HALLOWEEN THRILLER**

Donald **TRUMP** *in* **GASLIGHT**

*TRAPPED IN A HOUSE WITH A PSYCHOPATH!*

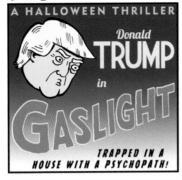

Mr. Trump, why are you adjusting the lights?

I'm not.

I just watched you do it. You just dimmed the lights.

No, I didn't. You must be going loco!

Are you trying to "gaslight" me? Play tricks on me so that I doubt my own sanity?

No, you are.

Because you're doing it wrong! It's not a trick if I watch you do it!

Yes, it is.

Oh my God! There's a dismembered journalist in this room!!

No, there's not.

And you're personally taking money from the murderer!

No, I'm not. I have nothing to do with him.

This isn't gaslighting! It's contradiction!

No, it's not.

What's that sound coming from the basement?

SHRIEK!! YOU'VE PUT CHILDREN IN CAGES!!

No, Obama did that.

I've got to get out of here... YAAAHHH! VLADIMIR PUTIN!

That's not Putin. Hillary is Putin's puppet.

Your lies are driving me crazy!

Gaslighting.

THAT'S NOT GASLIGHTING!

NEXT - 41% of the house's occupants agree with Trump: "Yes, it is."

10/22/18

TOM the DANCING BUG

by RUBEN BOLLING

## VOTING
### AN AMERICAN CHOICE!

DIST. BY ANDREWS McMEEL SYNDICATION ~ ©2018 R. BOLLING ~ 1411 ~ TO JOIN THE INNER HIVE, GO TO tomthedancingbug.com

10/29/18

# TOM the DANCING BUG'S
## SUPER-FUN-PAK COMIX
EDITED BY RUBEN BOLLING

DIST. BY ANDREWS McMEEL SYNDICATION - ©2018 R. Bolling -1412- TO JOIN THE INNER HIVE, GO TO tomthedancingbug.com

### CHICAGO PIZZA

MAN, CHICAGO HAS THE **BEST PIZZA**!

THAT'S NOT PIZZA. THAT'S A BOX OF PORN VHS TAPES.

OH, OKAY, MR. PIZZA SNOB.

### AH, LIFE

I'M SO DEPRESSED, DOCTOR.

YOU MUST GO SEE THE GREAT CLOWN PANNICHI!

AH, BUT YOU DON'T UNDERSTAND...

FOR THE LAST TIME, I'M NOT COMING TO YOUR CIRCUS SHOW, DR. PANNICHI!

HALF-OFF POPCORN COUPON?

### THE YEAR CHRISTMAS WAS CANCELED

THERE WILL BE NO CHRISTMAS THIS YEAR! MY DAD WAS TRANSFERRED TO CALIFORNIA!

RING

HELLO? WHAT'S THAT? THE TRANSFER'S OFF, AND WE CAN STAY IN THE NORTH POLE?!

CHRISTMAS IS BACK ON! Merry Christmas!!

### SCIENCE FACTS FOR THE MISOPHONIC

THE SOUND OF A HOARY MARMOT CHEWING ON A BOTTLEBRUSH SEDGE SEED CAN REACH SOUND LEVELS OF UP TO **35** DISGUSTING AND INFURIATING DECIBELS!

CRUNCH · SMACK · GNAW · CHOMP

### HOW TO DRAW DOUG

IT'S E-Z! JUST FOLLOW THESE SIMPLE STEPS!

❶ DRAW TWO INTERLOCKING OVALS

❷ CHECK EMAIL

❸ ADD TWO CIRCLES

❹ CHECK TWITTER NOTIFICATIONS

❺ BETTER CHECK EMAILS AGAIN
❻ ANYTHING ON REDDIT?
❼ GOOGLE THE KID ON MR. BELVEDERE
❽ TWITTER
❾ LOOK AT THE STREETVIEW OF YOUR GIR CONT'D

### AVATAR, THE COMIC STRIP

AND NOW I SHALL RETURN TO THE LAND OF AVATAR!

WOW, IT'S SURE BEEN A LONG TIME!

WELCOME BACK! I AM AVATAR!

WAIT, THERE'S A GUY NAMED AVATAR? I BARELY REMEMBER ALL THIS!

NEITHER DOES THE WRITER OF THIS COMIC STRIP! BUT IT IS OUR DUTY TO CONTINUE THE JOURNEY!

FOR HOW LONG?

IT MATTERS NOT! THROUGH MANY SEQUELS!

POW

WHEN YOU BOUGHT A TICKET TO THE AVATAR MOVIE IN 2009, YOU ENTERED A SACRED AND ETERNAL BOND WITH THE JAMES CAMERON!

CONTINUED!!

11/5/18

# TOM the DANCING BUG

by RUBEN BOLLING

## DoNald and JOHN
### a boy PrEsident and his Imaginary Publicist

DIST. BY ANDREWS MCMEEL SYNDICATION – ©2018 R. BOLLING – 1413 – TO JOIN THE INNER HIVE, GO TO tomthedancingbug.com

11/12/18

# TOM THE DANCING BUG

### SAVING PRESIDENT TRUMP

by RUBEN BOLLING

DIST. BY ANDREWS McMEEL SYNDICATION — ©2018 R BOLLING — 1414 · patreon.com/rubenbolling

Dear Mom,

I know it will be hard at the Thanksgiving table without me. But I'm where my country needs me.

Life here at the Texas border can be rough. Why, just today, the sarge called me over...

Reporting for duty, sir.

At ease, soldier. I've got a mission for you.

Special Ops needs barbed wire across this line.

Why would Special Operations need it there? Is the caravan of migrants approaching?

Not OPERATIONS! PHOTO OPS! The media is there!

Get nine of your best men and get out there! Five will lay wire, and five will provide cover.

Cover?! Are we expecting resistance?

No, POLITICAL cover for President Trump, you moron!

I've had enough of your lip! When you enlisted, you knew a soldier's sacred duty is to serve as a prop for President Trump's political strategies!

Well, I did sign up for tactical optics training.

And optics is exactly what we are providing!

RING!

Okay, I've got new marching orders for you.

I'm ready for any fighting challenge, sir.

No, you're ACTUALLY MARCHING! In Trump's gala military parade! What do you know about float design?

Say hey to Dad and little Sarah for me. Don't worry none -- if anything happens to me while in the parade, you can be sure President Trump will be there to honor my memory, weather and hair products permitting.

Your loving son, Henry

11/19/18

# TOM the DANCING BUG
## PRESENTS:

BY RUBEN BOLLING

## NEWS of the TIMES

## Scientists: Doomsday Asteroid to Hit Earth in June

### GOP: We Feel Like It Won't

NASA ANNOUNCED THE DISCOVERY OF A NINE-MILE-WIDE ASTEROID ON AN IMMINENT COLLISION COURSE WITH EARTH.

OUR CALCULATIONS ARE UNASSAILABLE! IF NOT DIVERTED, THIS ASTEROID WILL DESTROY ALL ADVANCED LIFE ON EARTH!

PFFT! CHECK OUT POINDEXTER HERE! WHAT B.S.-- I'LL TRADE HIS FANCY MATH FOR GOOD OL' COMMON SENSE ANY DAY!

DR. HOWARD JERROLD, SR. PLANETARY SCIENTIST, NASA

JOHN "BUD" HANDELSEN, SPOKESMAN, PATRIOT FREEDOM INSTITUTE, PRESENT TO PROVIDE POLITICAL BALANCE

OUR ONLY HOPE IS TO LAUNCH A NUCLEAR-ARMED ROCKET TO MEET THE ASTEROID AND CHANGE ITS COURSE! BUT WE MUST BEGIN IMMEDIATELY!

DR. SVEN FARVGEL, COLUMBIA ASTRO-PHYSICS LABORATORY

SOUNDS LIKE ELITIST FAKE NEWS TO ME! IF THERE'S AN ASTEROID, HOW COME I CAN'T SEE IT?

AND IF I DO SEE IT, I'LL JUST TAKE CARE OF IT WITH *PROFESSOR SMITH* AND *DR. WESSON* HERE!

REP. PAUL T. HARTON, R-TX.

*FOR THE LOVE OF GOD, WE HAVE PRECIOUS LITTLE TIME!* **I HAVE CHILDREN!**

DR. HAROLD FORSYTHE, M.I.T. PROFESSOR OF ASTRONAUTICS

**Donald J. Trump** ✓
@realDonaldTrump
Why should we build a rocket just so we can save a bunch of Mexicans and Chinese? #AmericaFirst #BuildTheWall #LockHerUp

OF COURSE SCIENTISTS WANT TO BUILD A ROCKET! THAT'S HOW THEY GET RICH!

SENATOR, THE CHECK FROM P.F.I. JUST CAME IN!

*NOT NOW!*

SEN. PETE ANSEL, R-KY.

NO WASTE MONEY ON ROCKET! NO ASTEROID! WILL NO KILL ALL MAMMALS.

KNOTT A. COCKROACH BILLIONAIRE G.O.P. DONOR, FOUNDER, PATRIOT FREEDOM INSTITUTE

11/26/18

12/3/18

TOM the DANCING BUG

by RUBEN BOLLING

DIST. BY ANDREWS McMEEL SYNDICATION – ©2018 R. BOLLING – 1417 – TO JOIN THE INNER HIVE, GO TO tomthedancingbug.com

# SCIENTIFIC GIANTS OF ALL TIME

*This week~* DONALD TRUMP'S GUT

There have been many scientific geniuses whose leaps of insight and tireless experimentation have transformed our lives, but perhaps none so intellectually gifted as Donald Trump's ample gut. Let us review the prodigious career of this most accomplished abdomen.

**1952** JONAS SALK IS WALKING BY A FOREST HILLS, Ny. PLAYGROUND WHEN HE OVERHEARS DONALD TRUMP'S GUT'S ASTONISHING HYPOTHESIS.

Subjecting a polio virus with a solution of formaldehyde at 1°c for 7-13 days would yield a robust antibody inducement.

GIMME YOUR LUNCH!

**1972** STEPHEN HAWKING IS AT A QUEENS STREETCORNER WHEN HE HAPPENS UPON DONALD TRUMP'S GUT MUSING ABOUT THE COSMOS.

SO IF THE FAMILY IS COLORED, PUT A "C" ON THE APPLICATION SO WE'LL KNOW TO REJECT THEM.

Does it not follow from quantum theory and relativity that black holes must emit radiation?

AHA!

**1996** JEFF KIMBLE IS IN A SHREVEPORT, La. HOTEL WHEN HE HEARS DONALD TRUMP'S GUT MAKE A STARTLING PROPOSAL.

MISS USA LOCKER ROOM

I'M COMING IN, GIRLS!

LOBBY

MISS USA PAGEANT ←

PHYSICS CONFERENCE →

Working with triplets of charged atoms, it would be possible to actually teleport a photon.

**2018** AND JUST THIS YEAR, DONALD TRUMP'S GUT HAS CONTINUED TO ASTOUND OUR GREATEST THINKERS.

You're all quite wrong about anthropogenic climate change. In your calculations, you forgot to carry the two!

IT'S A WITCH HUNT! SO UNFAIR!

WHA...?

HIS GUT IS RIGHT!

CLIMATOLOGIST CONVENTION

Many scoffed when Donald Trump's gut told him that Global Warming is a hoax. But now that it has been proven correct yet again, we must acknowledge the great debt of gratitude we owe to a true Giant of Science, ***Donald Trump's gut!***

12/10/18

TOM the DANCING BUG

by RUBEN BOLLING

Dr. Paul Ryan

**Fiscal Scientist**

DIST. BY ANDREWS McMEEL SYNDICATION — ©2018 R. BOLLING — 14.18 — TO JOIN THE INNER HIVE, GO TO tomthedancingbug.com

Hi, kids! I'm known as a wonk, so today we're going to run a real science experiment, with junior scientist Emily here!

Ready, Dr. Ryan!

It is my hypothesis that tax cuts for the rich grow the economy and create a budget surplus!

Let's test it, using science!

Here is a state called Kansas. We'll douse it with tax cuts for the rich and see what happens.

Um, Dr. Ryan, it's doing terribly.

Sorry, Emily, I couldn't hear you because I'm getting ready for the next experiment. Keep up.

Here is California, and it's in bad shape. Let's douse it in tax increases for the rich and see how much worse it gets.

Gosh! Dr. Ryan, it's doing great!

Emily, you're getting bogged down by details.

Now that we've rigorously proven my hypothesis, let's douse the whole U.S.A. in tax cuts for the rich and watch a budget surplus grow!

Hey! I live there!

Oh, no, Dr. Ryan! The budget's starting to bust... Hey, where are you going?!

I'm retiring, a HERO OF FISCAL SCIENCE!

NEXT: Getting paid by the rich for doing such awesome science!

12/17/18

# TOM the DANCING BUG'S

### EDITED BY RUBEN BOLLING

# SUPER-FUN-PAK COMIX

## COMICS APPROPRIATING AND ABUSING INTELLECTUAL PROPERTY NEWLY LAPSED INTO THE PUBLIC DOMAIN ON 1/1/19

### FRANKENSTEIN'S CASTLE

THAT BUILDING IN THE DISTANCE -- IT'S FRANKENSTEIN!

ACTUALLY, IT'S FRANKENSTEIN'S *CASTLE!* FRANKENSTEIN IS THE NAME OF THE *MONSTER!*

IT TRUE! *ME* FRANKENSTEIN!

### EMIL THE BACTERIUM PHYSICIST

The math works out! There must be more to the Universe than this pile of raccoon feces!

But Emil, it is so unfathomably vast! What could be beyond it?

Perhaps other kinds of raccoon feces that we cannot even conceive of.

Wow.

### DOUG: INTO THE DOUGVERSE

Hi, I'm DOUG FROM an ALTERNATE UNIVERSE!

YOU DON'T SEEM DIFFERENT AT ALL.

WELL, LET'S SEE...

Um, Do you Like FRENCH TOAST?

SURE.

WELL, I *LOVE* IT!

AH!

Hi, I ADORE FRENCH TOAST!

CONT'D

### CLASSIX COMIX

Not a substitute for reading the text or for classroom discussion of the text.

The Old Testament

I AM ALL-POWERFUL. WORSHIP ME.

O.K.

ACTUALLY, NAH.

WHAT A BUNCH OF JERKS.

OH, WELL. I'LL TRY AGAIN...

SPLAT!

### NOT A PIPE

This is not a pipe.

It is Frankenstein.

ACTUALLY, IT FRANKENSTEIN'S *PIPE!* ME FRANKENSTEIN!

"Whose woods these are I think I know.
His house is in the village though;
He will not see me stopping here
To watch his woods fill up with snow.

My little horse must think it queer
To stop without a farmhouse near
Between the woods and frozen lake
The darkest evening of the year.

He gives his harness bells a shake
To ask if there is some mistake.
The only other sound's the sweep
Of easy wind and downy flake.

The woods are lovely, dark and deep,
But I have promises to keep,
And miles to go before I sleep,
And miles to go while I fart."

"Who farted?"

DIST. BY ANDREWS McMEEL SYNDICATION - © 2019 R. Bolling -1419- TO JOIN THE INNER HIVE, GO TO tomthedancingbug.com

# TOM the DANCING BUG

by RUBEN BOLLING

## DONALD and JOHN
### a boy President and his Imaginary Publicist

DIST. BY ANDREWS McMEEL SYNDICATION — ©2019 R. BOLLING — 14-20 — TO JOIN THE INNER HIVE, GO TO tomthedancingbug.com

1/7/19

# TOM the DANCING BUG

PRESENTS:

BY RUBEN BOLLING

**N?WS of the TIM?S**

**Bombshell:**

## Trump Under Investigation

-

### Is He Disloyal to Russia?

DIST. BY ANDREWS McMEEL SYNDICATION — ©2019 R BOLLING — 1421 — TO JOIN THE INNER HIVE, GO TO tomthedancingbug.com

THE KREMLIN HAS BEEN INVESTIGATING WHETHER DONALD TRUMP IS TRULY LOYAL TO US, OR IF PERHAPS HE IS SECRETLY WORKING FOR THE AMERICANS.

WE HAD TRUMP IN-STALLED AS PRESIDENT AT CONSIDERABLE EXPENSE, AND HAD CERTAIN EXPECTATIONS.

IT MAY BE SHOCKING, BUT WE HAVE TO ASK: *IS THE U.S. PRESIDENT FULLY COMMITTED TO RUSSIA?*

RUSSIANS ARE GROWING IMPATIENT WITH TRUMP'S LACK OF PROGRESS.

I DIDN'T PRETEND TO BE A TUCSON HOUSEWIFE CONCERNED ABOUT HILLARY'S EMAILS FULL-TIME, FOR NINE MONTHS, FOR THIS ORANGE BABOON'S ASS TO FAIL TO LIFT ALL SANCTIONS.

I BOUGHT MANSION AND CONDO FROM THIS DEMENTED TURNIP, AND YET U.S. IS STILL MEMBER OF NATO. AM I IDIOT?

SURE, HE'S DONE GREAT DAMAGE TO THE U.S. BUT ALL *WE'VE* GOTTEN SO FAR IS SOME KIND WORDS ABOUT OUR INVASIONS.

TRUMP'S ATTEMPTS AT SUB-TERFUGE ARE SO MORONIC, MANY SUSPECT HE MAY HAVE BEEN PURPOSELY INCOMPE-TENT, TIPPING OFF U.S. AUTHORITIES.

RUSSIA, IF YOU'RE LISTENING, RELEASE HILLARY'S EMAILS.

NEVERTHELESS, THE FSB BELIEVES THAT TRUMP IS NOT DOUBLE-CROSSING THEM.

HE'S FOLLOWED ALL OUR INSTRUCTIONS. IT JUST HAPPENS THAT HE IS VERY, VERY STUPID.

WE'LL GIVE IT A COUPLE MORE MONTHS, AND IF WE DON'T SEE IMPROVEMENT, WE'LL HAVE THE BOYS IN R&D WHIP UP SOMETHING TO SLIP INTO HIS DIET COKE, AND THEN TRY AGAIN WITH THAT PENCE IDIOT.

1/14/19

1/21/19

TOM the DANCING BUG

by RUBEN BOLLING

DIST. BY ANDREWS McMEEL SYNDICATION — ©2019 R. BOLLING — 14-23 — TO JOIN THE INNER HIVE, GO TO tomthedancingbug.com

# CAN YOU SPOT THE DANGER?

**1. Can you spot the greatest risk of an extremist murder?**

**2. Can you spot the greatest probability of a deadly drug dealer?**

**3. Can you spot the greatest criminal threat?**

Answers:

1. The man in the MAGA hat is the greatest risk. 49 out of 50 extremist murders in 2018 were committed by domestic right-wing extremists.

2. The most dangerous drug dealer is the man in the suit, a salesman for OxyContin, who for years promoted its use to doctors as safe and non-addictive, contributing to an addiction epidemic that now kills about 130 Americans every day.

3. The greatest criminal threat is *the golfer*. The caddy is an undocumented immigrant, a group that is convicted of crimes at a rate of about 0.75%. The golfer, whose club illegally hired the caddy, was a key member of the 2016 Trump campaign, 19% of whom have been indicted or pled guilty to crimes.

So far.

1/28/19

# TOM the DANCING BUG'S SUPER-FUN-PAK COMIX
### EDITED BY RUBEN BOLLING

## PRAYERS ANSWERED

## LIFE CHOICES G.P.S.

## A MODEST PROPOSAL, Ltd.

## PERCIVAL DUNWOODY, IDIOT TIME TRAVELER FROM 1909

## CHAOS-BUTTERFLY-MAN

2/4/19

DIST. BY ANDREWS McMEEL SYNDICATION — ©2019 R. BOLLING — 14.25 — TO JOIN THE INNER HIVE, GO TO tomthedancingbug.com

2/11/19

DIST. BY ANDREWS McMEEL SYNDICATION – © 2019 R. BOLLING – 14.26 – TO JOIN THE INNER HIVE, GO TO tomthedancingbug.com

2/18/19

# COFFEE BEANS

featuring

## "Good ol' Howard Schultz"

### THE BILLIONAIRE PRESIDENTIAL CANDIDATE

DIST. BY ANDREWS McMEEL SYNDICATION ~ ©2019 R. BOLLING ~ 1427 ~ TO JOIN THE INNER HIVE, GO TO tomthedancingbug.com

2/25/19

# TOM the DANCING BUG

by RUBEN BOLLING

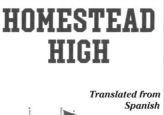

## HOMESTEAD HIGH

*Translated from Spanish*

HOMESTEAD BRANCH

GOSH, I HAVE A **DATE** TO LOOK ACROSS THE FIELD AND THROUGH THE FENCE TO MAKE EYE CONTACT WITH TWO DIFFERENT GIRLS AT THE SAME TIME!

HOW DO YOU GET YOURSELF INTO THESE MESSES?

I GUESS I'M JUST A TYPICAL TEEN IN A TYPICAL AMERICAN FOR-PROFIT CONCENTRATION CAMP!

WELL, I'LL HELP YOU FIGURE IT OUT!

THANKS, BUDDY!

HEY! NO TOUCHING ALLOWED!!

HI, MS. LUCEY! I SURE COULD USE SOME ADVICE! SEE, I MADE A...

TIME FOR MANDATORY OUTDOOR ACTIVITY! SINGLE FILE LINE, NOW!

GEE, IF YOU'RE MY TEACHER, HOW COME YOU NEVER TALK TO ME? OR TEACH?

MY CORPORATION DOESN'T MAKE MONEY TEACHING YOU! IT MAKES MONEY HOUSING YOU!

WE'RE ONLY SUPPOSED TO BE HOUSED IN THIS "TEMPORARY" FACILITY FOR THIRTY DAYS, BUT MANY OF US HAVE BEEN HERE FOR **MANY** MONTHS!

WELL, I'VE GOT GOOD NEWS FOR YOU THEN! YOU'RE GETTING **OUT**!

**GETTING OUT??** YOU'RE REUNITING ME WITH MY ADULT RELATIVES WHO CAME WITH ME TO THE U.S. TO APPLY FOR ASYLUM?

NOT EXACTLY...

TODAY'S YOUR **18TH BIRTHDAY**! WE'RE REMOVING YOU TO AN **ICE ADULT DETENTION CENTER**!

OH, BOY! GRADUATION DAY!

**Next** MORE HILARIOUS HIJINX *in* "HOMESTEAD ON ICE: THE ADULT YEARS"

DIST. BY ANDREWS McMEEL SYNDICATION — ©2019 R. BOLLING — 1428 — TO JOIN THE INNER HIVE, GO TO tomthedancingbug.com

3/4/19

DIST. BY ANDREWS McMEEL SYNDICATION ~ ©2019 R. BOLLING ~ 14-29 ~ TO JOIN THE INNER HIVE, GO TO tomthedancingbug.com

3/11/19

BY
RUBEN
BOLLING

NEWS OF THE TIMES

**College Admissions Scandal**

*Local Billionaire Caught in Bribery Scheme*

PROSECUTORS SAY THAT BILLIONAIRE AND PHILANTHROPIST HOLLINGSWORTH HOUND WAS CAUGHT BRIBING AN OFFICIAL OF THE PRESTIGIOUS COOT UNIVERSITY TO ADMIT HIS SON.

IT IS ESSENTIAL THAT THE PUBLIC KNOW THAT ILLEGAL BRIBERY HAS NO PLACE IN THE PURE MERITOCRACY THAT GOVERNS OUR ELITE EDUCATIONAL INSTITUTIONS!

DISTRICT ATTORNEY BENNETT BEAGLE

DIST. BY ANDREWS McMEEL SYNDICATION – © 2019 R. BOLLING – 1430 – TO JOIN THE INNER HIVE, GO TO tomthedancingbug.com

MR. HOUND'S ATTORNEYS QUICKLY REFUTED THE CHARGE.

THIS IS AN OUTRAGEOUS ACCUSATION! MR. HOUND WAS MERELY BRIBING *COOT UNIVERSITY* TO ADMIT HIS SON!

A VIDEO OF THE MEETING EMERGED, AND IT SHOWS THAT THE TRANSACTION STARTED ON FULLY LEGAL GROUNDS.

HERE IS MY $20 MILLION DONATION TO COOT UNIVERSITY.

AND HERE IS HOLLINGSWORTH IV'S ADMISSION LETTER.

3:13pm

BUT THEN THE MEETING TOOK A BRAZEN, SHOCKINGLY ILLEGAL TURN!

AND HERE'S $50 FOR YOUR TROUBLE. GO BUY YOURSELF SOMETHING NICE!

3:14pm

PROSECUTORS WERE TRIUMPHANT.

JUST AFTER THE $20 MILLION GIFT AND ADMISSIONS ACCEPTANCE, MR. HOUND SUBVERTED ALL OF HIGHER EDUCATION BY PAYING AN INDIVIDUAL 50 BUCKS FOR FAVORITISM!

I... ER... WASN'T BRIBING THE UNIVERSITY PRESIDENT! I WAS BRIBING THE *UNIVERSITY*! HONEST!

BUT AFTER MAKING A PERFECTLY LEGAL CONTRIBUTION TO THE D.A.'S RE-ELECTION CAMPAIGN, MR. HOUND SAW ALL CHARGES AGAINST HIM COINCIDENTALLY DROPPED!

THE SYSTEM WORKS! I LEARNED SO MUCH!

NO MORE TIPPING, RIGHT, POP?

3/18/19

# TOM the DANCING BUG'S
EDITED BY RUBEN BOLLING

# SUPER-FUN-PAK COMIX

## LADY-SUPERHERO-MAN

BITTEN BY A RADIO-ACTIVE LADY SUPER-HERO, HAL HARRIS GAINED THE POWERS OF A LADY SUPERHERO!

STOP! I HAVE SUPER-STRENGTH AND LASER-BLAST EYES!

AH, SEEMS IMPLAUSIBLE.

ARGH! IT'S TRUE! MY POWERS ARE MERE DIVERSITY TOKENISM!

YOU SHOULD SMILE MORE!

## EMIL THE BACTERIUM PHYSICIST

According to my calculations, this raccoon feces sprang into existence 117 hours ago, then dropped 8 inches.

The immense distance and time are inconceivable! But it dropped from *where*?

That's a metaphysical question that my Big Bung Theory cannot answer.

## AH, LIFE

DOCTOR, I'M SO DEPRESSED.

TREATMENT IS SIMPLE. GO SEE GREAT CLOWN PANNICHI!

O.K.

TELL ME ABOUT YOUR MOTHER.

Moore

## SCHRÖDINGER'S CAT AND THEIR WACKY FRIEND WIGNER

AS LONG AS I'M UNOBSERVED IN THIS BOX, I CAN SIMULTANEOUSLY NAP AND EAT PIZZA!

DON'T YOU HATE WHEN SOMEONE RUINS A NAP?

## THE ADVENTURES OF ACTUALLY-MAN

AAIEE! IT'S FRANKENSTEIN!

ACTUALLY, IT'S FRANKENSTEIN'S *MONSTER*.

ACTUALLY, IN THE ORIGINAL NOVEL, I NAME MYSELF *ADAM*.

**META, BUT NOT META ENOUGH**

"Sigh."

DIST. BY ANDREWS McMEEL SYNDICATION - © 2019 R. Bolling - 1431 - TO JOIN THE INNER HIVE, GO TO tomthedancingbug.com

DIST. BY ANDREWS McMEEL SYNDICATION ~ ©2019 R.BOLLING ~ 1432 ~ TO JOIN THE INNER HIVE, GO TO tomthedancingbug.com

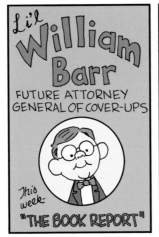

Li'l William Barr

FUTURE ATTORNEY GENERAL OF COVER-UPS

This week:

"THE BOOK REPORT"

LI'L WILLIAM, PLEASE COME TO THE FRONT OF THE CLASS AND GIVE YOUR **BOOK REPORT**.

AHEM. "**OF MICE AND MEN**" DOES NOT DEFINITIVELY ESTABLISH THAT LENNIE KILLED CURLEY'S WIFE.

NOR DOES IT EXONERATE HIM.

LI'L WILLIAM, THIS IS JUST LIKE YOUR REPORT ON "**MOBY-DICK**."

WELL, EVIDENCE THAT THE WHALE BIT OFF AHAB'S LEG FAILED TO MEET MY BURDEN OF PROOF.

AND YOUR REPORT ON "**1984**"?

ORWELL LEFT IT TO THE READER TO DECIDE WHETHER **BIG BROTHER** COMMITTED ABUSES OF POWER, AND **I** DECIDED HE **DIDN'T**.

LI'L WILLIAM, I'M WRITING A NOTE TO YOUR PARENTS. BE SURE TO GIVE IT TO THEM.

Dear Mr. and Mrs. Ba
Li'l William only skims the assigned works and then tortuously cherry-picks and manipulates the text to support his wildl inappropriate conclusions.
John

THAT NIGHT~

LI'L WILLIAM, IS THAT YOUR REPORT CARD? LET US SEE IT.

NO, YOU **CAN'T** SEE IT, BUT I'LL **SUMMARIZE** IT FOR YOU: IT STRESSES THAT I COMPLETE MY ASSIGNMENTS, AND CONTAINS SEVERAL INSTANCES OF THE LETTER "**A**."

The End

4/1/19

# TOM the DANCING BUG

by RUBEN BOLLING

## WHO ACKNOWLEDGES THAT CLIMATE CHANGE IS A REALITY?

## AND WHO DOESN'T?

4/8/19

# TOM the DANCING BUG

by RUBEN BOLLING

## DONALD and JOHN

### a boy President and his Imaginary Publicist

DIST. BY ANDREWS McMEEL SYNDICATION – ©2019 R. BOLLING – 1434 – TO JOIN THE INNER HIVE, GO TO tomthedancingbug.com

4/15/19

TOM the DANCING BUG

by RUBEN BOLLING

"THE SPECIAL COUNSEL OF OZ"

DIST. BY ANDREWS McMEEL SYNDICATION – ©2019 R. BOLLING – 1435 – TO JOIN THE INNER HIVE, GO TO tomthedancingbug.com

4/22/19

TOM the DANCING BUG

by RUBEN BOLLING

DIST. BY ANDREWS McMEEL SYNDICATION – ©2019 R.BOLLING – 1436 – TO JOIN THE INNER HIVE, GO TO tomthedancingbug.com

# DONALD TRUMP'S GUIDE TO FINE PEOPLE

No one knows more about Fine People than me, so I've decided to rank the Fine People throughout history!

## CHARLOTTESVILLE MARCHERS

Many people were there to protest the removal of a historic statue of General Lee, who was a great general, everyone knows it.

VERY FINE PEOPLE 👍👍👍

## KRISTALLNACHT RIOTERS

There were some rotten apples, but many were simply protesting local zoning laws that allowed too many glass storefronts.

QUITE FINE PEOPLE 👍👍

## LYNCHERS

Things often got out of hand, but many who were there were just trying to showcase their sheet-based crafting projects.

REALLY FINE PEOPLE 👍

## FAMILY SEPARATORS

Thousands of Latin American families have been shattered and destroyed, but those behind the policy only wanted to shatter and destroy Latin American families.

BIGLY FINE PEOPLE 👍👍👍👍

4/29/19

TOM the DANCING BUG

by RUBEN BOLLING

DIST. BY ANDREWS McMEEL SYNDICATION – ©2019 R. BOLLING – 1438 – TO JOIN THE INNER HIVE, GO TO tomthedancingbug.com

## Georgia's new "LIFE" Act is an absolute benefit for its women!

Yes, there are a few draconian, unconstitutional provisions prohibiting abortions, but by defining every fetus and embryo, no matter how microscopic, as a "person," it creates *great opportunities for pregnant ladies!*

### Who's Zoomin' Who?
From the moment of conception, a woman can use the HOV lane when driving "alone" because that little zygote counts as another passenger!

### Premium Seating!
No car? No problem! Go ahead and spread out on that bus, because two "persons" are entitled to two seats, right?

### Dining Delights!
Eating at one of Georgia's great restaurants that offer a kids-eat-free deal? You can order a kids' meal for that blastocyst, and treat it as a free app for you!

### Get out of Jail Free!
Feel like committing a crime? Well, the state can't put you in prison because doing so would deprive the innocent "person" floating in your uterus of its own liberty!

### You're welcome, lucky ladies!
And look, if you really have a problem with your pregnancy, you can always call that multi-celled "person" who suddenly showed up inside you a HOME INVADER and use Georgia's "Stand Your Ground" laws to take care of business!

Wait... What?

Quit yer frettin', females! We know this new law will make all the ladies say...

*"Georgia is on my mind!"*

5/13/19

THE PERFECT CANDIDATE TO BEAT TRUMP

TOM the DANCING BUG

by RUBEN BOLLING

DIST. BY ANDREWS McMEEL SYNDICATION – ©2019 R. BOLLING – 1439 – TO JOIN THE INNER HIVE, GO TO tomthedancingbug.com

**2019** Biden's a great candidate because he's center-right. So he'll get votes from every voter to his left.

But, wait! We can do better! Let's find someone even closer to Trump!

Then we'll get all the votes to the left of *that* guy! I found some-one! Ronald Hump, of Staten Island, New York!

## HUMP 2020 DEMOCRATIC NOMINEE

Slightly less orange hue

Wants to pack courts with slightly fewer radical judges who will overturn Roe v. Wade

Thinks Climate Change is a Chinese fire drill

Demands a big, but slightly less beautiful, wall

Treasonous secret relationship with the leader of Turkey, who is slightly less venal than Putin

Believes migrant children should be put in slightly nicer cages

Would go to war with Iran only over a slightly greater pretense than the sabotage of Saudi tankers

Lifetime tax fraud total is only $300 million

Settled with prosecutors for racial discrimination in only 15 rental buildings

Only 19 women have accused him of sexual assault

**2020** I don't get it! Hump lost to Trump! Under our theory, Hump should have gotten 120 million votes! He got... ZERO!

You didn't vote for him either? Hell, no! Hump's a monster!

I won't concede! I would have won, but there was slightly less than MASSIVE VOTER FRAUD!

5/20/19

# TOM the DANCING BUG'S
## SUPER-FUN-PAK COMIX
EDITED BY RUBEN BOLLING

DIST. BY ANDREWS McMEEL SYNDICATION - ©2019 R. Bolling - 1440- TO JOIN THE INNER HIVE, GO TO tomthedancingbug.com

### ANTHROPOMORPHIC CLIMATE CHANGE

I JUST DON'T BELIEVE IN IT! I'M A SKEPTIC!

JEEZ, HE'S RIGHT BEHIND YOU!

HOW RUDE!

### PERCIVAL DUNWOODY, IDIOT TIME TRAVELER FROM 1909

I SHALL GO BACK IN TIME AND TAKE YOUR ICE CREAM FROM YOU.

THERE. NOW WE CAN BOTH HAVE ONE.

THAT MAKES NO SENSE.

AH, BUT I AM AN IDIOT.

### AH, LIFE

DOCTOR, ME SO DEPRESSED!

FRANKENSTEIN IS PERFORMING IN TOWN! GO SEE HIM!

YOU NO UNDERSTAND! me FRANKENSTEIN!

ACTUALLY, YOU'RE FRANKENSTEIN'S **monster!**

THAT NO HELP!

### WALTER-HIGGINS-MAN

SO, YOU WERE BITTEN BY WALTER HIGGINS, FROM ACCOUNTING?

WHILE HE WAS RADIOACTIVE?

YEAH.

SO, WHAT ARE YOUR POWERS?

I'M RATHER GOOD AT BUMPER POOL, AND I KNOW A LOT ABOUT '80s POP MUSIC.

SORRY AGAIN ABOUT BITING YOU.

THAT'S OKAY, WALTER. I'M ALSO PRETTY POLITE.

### NO GAYS IN THIS COMIC FOR KIDS

Yay, my teacher is getting married!

It's good that you're marrying a lady, Mr. Howard!

Yes, it's important for you to know that I put my penis into vaginas only.

## HOW TO DRAW DOUG

BOLLING

① BUILD A LARGE HADRON COLLIDER.

② COLLIDE PROTON BEAMS, CREATING MINIATURE BLACK HOLES.

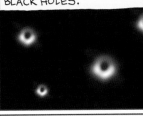

③ USE A BLACK HOLE AS A PORTAL INTO A PARALLEL UNIVERSE IN WHICH YOU HAVE THE INNATE ABILITY TO DRAW DOUG, A SKILL YOU'VE ALREADY HONED THROUGH TENS OF THOUSANDS OF HOURS OF TIRELESS PRACTICE.

④ DRAW DOUG.

VOILÀ!

5/27/19

# TOM the DANCING BUG

by RUBEN BOLLING

DIST. BY ANDREWS McMEEL SYNDICATION – ©2019 R. BOLLING – 1441 – TO JOIN THE INNER HIVE, GO TO tomthedancingbug.com

**PERPLEXED** BY MUELLER'S ENIGMATIC STATEMENTS?

**CONFUSED** BY HIS MUDDLED CONCLUSIONS?

Yes, Special Counsel Robert Mueller so constrained himself with his interpretation of Department of Justice policies that he can only speak about his own report IN CODE!

*But now you can decipher this code* **with the new...**

# MUELLER DECODER!!

Simply enter Mueller's reticent, circuitous statement into the Mueller Decoder, and you'll discover his actual meaning!

---

If we didn't fail to find that the President didn't not commit a crime, we would not refuse to say so.

Gosh, the President committed a crime!! | Good thing we have our Mueller Decoder!

---

While a Nixon administration policy precludes us from charging the President with a crime, the Constitution houses another process to do so.

Golly, he is referring the charges to the House of Representatives for Impeachment!

---

There were multiple, systematic efforts to interfere with our election. And that allegation deserves the attention of every American.

... E... L...P. What does that spell out? | "Good lord, Mitch McConnell is blocking all attempts to protect our elections! Help!"

---

**ACT NOW,** *and you'll also get a* **TRUMP DECODER!!**

Those who defy me will be arrested by my own personal Justice Department for Treason.

What does it translate to? | "Look behind you."

6/3/19

DIST. BY ANDREWS McMEEL SYNDICATION — ©2019 R. BOLLING — 1442 — TO JOIN THE INNER HIVE, GO TO tomthedancingbug.com

6/10/19

# TOM the DANCING BUG

PRESENTS:

BY
RUBEN
BOLLING

## NEWS of the TIMES

## Trump Welcomes Russian Ground Troops into U.S.A.

IN WHAT SOME CRITICS ARE CALLING AN "INVASION," RUSSIAN FORCES HAVE ENTERED THE U.S. AND SEIZED CONTROL OF MILITARY BASES AND GOVERNMENT BUILDINGS. PRESIDENT TRUMP ANGRILY DENIES THAT CHARACTERIZATION.

NOT AN INVASION. NO INVASION. ALL THE BEST PEOPLE ARE SAYING IT'S NOT AN ANNEXATION.

IN A CONTROVERSIAL MOVE, TRUMP NAMED VLADIMIR PUTIN CHANCELLOR OF THE UNITED STATES.

I HAPPEN TO THINK HAVING A BETTER RELATIONSHIP WITH PUTIN IS A **GOOD** THING!

TRUMP'S APPROVAL RATING DROPPED ONLY TWO POINTS, TO 39%.

GOD BLESS DONALD TRUMP. LET THE SNOW-FLAKES WHINE ABOUT WHICH RUSSIAN TROOPS ARE RAPING THIS OR PILLAGING THAT.

COINCIDENTALLY, JUST PRIOR TO THE RUSSIAN TROOPS' ARRIVAL, A RUSSIAN OLIGARCH BOUGHT A CONDO FROM TRUMP FOR $2.6 MILLION.

HERE ARE THE "KEYS."

SERIOUSLY? THIS ALL IT TAKES? IS VERY CHEAP!

ROBERT MUELLER WAS ENLISTED TO INVESTIGATE THE ALLEGATION THAT TRUMP IS A TRAITOR, AND THEN SUBMITTED HIS REPORT.

I REFER TO FOOTNOTE 273: IF WE FOUND NO TREASON, WE WOULD NOT DECLINE TO NOT...

NO TRAITOR! NO TREASON! WITCH HUNT! NEXT!

BELIEVE ME, DEMOCRATS WOULD DO THE SAME THING. *WE DEMONSTRABLY WOULD NOT!*

R33DUCAT CAMP

DIST. BY ANDREWS McMEEL SYNDICATION – ©2019 R.BOLLING – 1443 – TO JOIN THE INNER HIVE, GO TO tomthedancingbug.com

'6/17/19

TOM the DANCING BUG

by RUBEN BOLLING

DIST. BY ANDREWS McMEEL SYNDICATION – ©2019 R. BOLLING – 1444 – TO JOIN THE INNER HIVE, GO TO tomthedancingbug.com

# PLEASE REMEMBER THE "CONCENTRATION CAMP" VICTIMS

It's horrifying but true. In the United States today, Republicans in Congress are subjected to having the migrant detention centers they support called "concentration camps." We call on all good Americans to end this humanitarian travesty.

I never thought this could happen to me in my own country.

To hurt my feelings by referring to this as a concentration camp is simply criminal.
I may never be the same.

The degradation. The nightmares. And I'll never get an apology!

Señor, este niño está muy enfermo.

FACT: "Concentration camp" is defined as a detention center holding persecuted minorities in crowded conditions and inadequate facilities, PRESIDED OVER BY A GUY WITH A HITLER MUSTACHE.

NO HITLER MUSTACHE = NO CONCENTRATION CAMP!

Words can hurt just as much as inhumane sleep deprivation, persistent hunger, and untreated influenza. Only much more so.

## YOU CAN HELP!

**Surely you can put aside partisan allegiances and respond with compassion and humanity!**

☐ For just $5 per month you can sustain Congressional staff tweets expressing outrage at the nomenclature used for the torture and killing of children.
☐ For just $100 per month you can help maintain a Republican congressperson's paying job after 2020.
☐ For just $200 per month you can get some kind of tax reduction or regulatory break for your business. Whatever, *just ask.*

Send your check or money order to the Republican Party today and end this needless suffering.

6/24/19

# TOM the DANCING BUG'S SUPER-FUN-PAK COMIX
### EDITED BY RUBEN BOLLING

### CHEKHOV'S GUM

ACT 1 — WANT SOME BUBBLICIOUS? / NO, THANKS.

ACT 2 — ARE YOU SURE? / WELL...

ACT 3

### YESTERDAY: THE BOARD GAME

Gasp! I'm the only person who remembers The Beatles!

Why would we publish a board game based on something called The Beatles?

### GOOD COP / BETTER COP / BEST COP

YOU'D BETTER TALK, OR I'LL BRING IN MY PARTNERS!

HI, I MADE YOU SALTED CARAMEL BLONDIES!

WE CAN GET IN ONE MORE RIDE BEFORE OUR RESERVATION AT THE LIBERTY TREE.

### PIXAR'S "OFFICE SUPPLY STORY"

DAVIS, GET IN HERE! / I'LL BE RIGHT THERE!

HELP! I'M ALIVE! / AUGGH! / WHY? WHY? / IT... IS... HELL!

### KAFKAESQUE NIGHTMARE

What's this? Something's wrong!

Good lord!

Hey, what's... / It's a pimple, okay?!! On picture day!

DIST. BY ANDREWS McMEEL SYNDICATION - ©2019 R. Bolling -1446- TO JOIN THE INNER HIVE, GO TO tomthedancingbug.com

7/8/19

7/15/19

# DoNald and JoHN
## a boy PrEsident and his Imaginary Publicist

THE FOUR GIRLS IN THIS SQUAD ARE SO **YUCKY!** THEY HATE AMERICA!

HOW DO YOU KNOW?

THEY DON'T THINK AMERICA IS GREAT!

LET'S GO TO YOUR CAMPAIGN ROOM TO FIGURE OUT HOW TO RESPOND TO THEM.

GOOD IDEA.

I MEAN WHO WOULD EVER DARE SAY AMERICA IS NOT GREAT?!

AMERICA GREAT AGAIN

MAKE AMERICA GREAT AGAIN

MAGA

ALEXANDRIA, YOU'RE YUCKY, AND YOU'LL NEVER BE A TRUE AMERICAN.!

CaNdid OpiNioNs

**GO BACK TO WHERE YOU CAME FROM!**

CaNdid OpiNioNs

NOT ONLY IS THAT AN UNAMERICAN THING TO SAY, BUT UNLIKE **YOU**, IT HAPPENS THAT BOTH OF **MY** PARENTS WERE BORN AMERICAN CITIZENS!

YEAH, BUT MY **SKIN COLOR'S** BEEN AMERICAN LONGER THAN YOURS!

I THOUGHT BRIGHT ORANGE IS A **NEW** SKIN COLOR

CaNdid OpiNioNs

SEND HER BACK! SEND HER BACK! SEND

SEND HER BACK! SEND HER BACK! SEND HER BACK

I THINK THEY'RE DONE.

VERY BRAVE OF YOU TO STOP THEM, DONALD!

YOU'RE IN TROUBLE FOR RACIST TWEETS!

THEN I'LL DISTRACT 'EM WITH A TWEET ABOUT RUSSIA!

NOW YOU'RE IN TROUBLE FOR WHAT YOU SAID ABOUT RUSSIAN COLLUSION!

THEN I'LL DISTRACT 'EM WITH THE SEX ASSAULT ISSUE!

**NOW** YOU'RE IN TROUBLE FOR YOUR SEX ASSAULT ISSUE!

THEN I'LL DISTRACT 'EM WITH A RACIST TWEET!

THAT'S WHAT YOU STARTED TRYING TO DISTRACT PEOPLE **FROM!**

SO WHAT? IT'S THE DISTRACTING THAT MATTERS!

7/22/19

# TOM the DANCING BUG

by RUBEN BOLLING

Former Special Counsel Robert Mueller's Congressional testimony that Donald Trump welcomed, received, and used Russian assistance in his campaign was a disaster for Democrats because he looked old on TV.

This brought to mind the speeches of World War II, and how cable TV pundits shaped our perception of its momentous events.

DIST. BY ANDREWS McMEEL SYNDICATION – ©2019 R. BOLLING – 1449 – TO JOIN THE INNER HIVE, GO TO tomthedancingbug.com

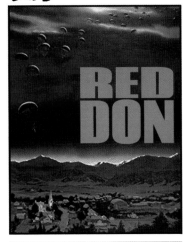

TOM the DANCING BUG

by RUBEN BOLLING

**RED DON**

I can't believe the Russians invaded America!

Good thing we kids hid up here in the woods!

We need to fight back!!

Yeah! WOLVERINES!!

As leader of our renegade crew of patriotic teenagers, I say, NO!!

Huh?

How do we know it's even the Russians? It could have been anybody!

Um, we saw them.

Why did we elect this guy to be our leader anyway?

Oh, because these typical Americans said he's great!

Da! He is the very good!

That is right, Lisa483372!

So cool your jets, dudes!

Is there another leader of our group who will do something to stop the Russians??

Uh... Nope.

Ah, it's obvious this guy's a traitor! We need to kick him out!

Yeah!!

Not so fast! That wouldn't be strategic!

Oh, Nancy.

Oh, forget it. I'm heading back to town for some borscht and Russian lessons.

8/5/19

# TOM the DANCING BUG

by RUBEN BOLLING

DIST. BY ANDREWS McMEEL SYNDICATION ~ ©2019 R. BOLLING ~ 1451 ~ TO JOIN THE INNER HIVE, GO TO tomthedancingbug.com

## ATTENTION CITIZENS OF LATINO NATIONS

# HELP WANTED   AQUÍ HAY TRABAJO

*Come to America!!*

Jefe Donald Trump

**T R U M P**
THE TRUMP ORGANIZATION

**Suffering** from economic hardship?

**Want** a better life?

**Sneak** into the United States!

I will secretly and illegally hire you in America for my construction projects or golf clubs or other businesses *because you will work cheaper than American workers!*

---

**FULL DISCLOSURE**
- I will publicly call you an invader and an infestation and a thug and an animal.
- Trump managers will threaten to report you to the authorities so that you'll work extra hours for free.

**FULLER DISCLOSURE**
- After you build a life here in America, I'll rip your family apart. Your children will be left devastated and alone.
- I will suffer NO CONSEQUENCES for breaking the law and actually CREATING, with my buddies, the entire system of undocumented immigration.

---

*Yes, the Trump Organization employs undocumented workers!*
Throughout my campaign, throughout my presidency, and to this very day!
*Is the hypocrisy breathtaking?* You bet!!

**MY GUARANTEE**
*You* take the risks!
*Trump* takes the profits!

**TRUMP'S AMERICA**

You'll **come** for the economic abuse!

You'll **stay** for the political abuse!

And then you'll **leave.**

8/12/19

# TOM the DANCING BUG

by RUBEN BOLLING

DIST. BY ANDREWS McMEEL SYNDICATION — ©2019 R. BOLLING — 1452 — TO JOIN THE INNER HIVE, GO TO tomthedancingbug.com

## DEPARTMENT OF JUSTICE
## TERRORISM DETECTIVE

I know there's one inspiration driving all this violence, but what is it?

WHAT?!

Boss, look! I analyzed the van owned by that mail bomber!

Whaddaya got?

**Panel 3:**
These stickers on the window are laid out in a rectangle roughly the shape of Afghanistan!

So it could be Al Qaeda! Good work! Keep looking!

**Panel 4:**
No leads on the Pittsburgh synagogue shooter's inspiration, boss.

Think! Think! Who promoted fear and hate with regard to an "invasion"?

**Panel 5:**
I've got it! The 1978 video game "Space Invaders"!

Video games! Of course! Find out if the designer of the game promoted any anti-Semitic Soros conspiracy theories!

**Panel 6:**
Anything on that guy in jail for death threats to Rep. Tlaib?

Let's see... one of the things he wrote: "don't tell our president, Donald Trump, what to say."

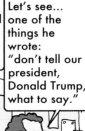

**Panel 7:**
Hold on! If you take the first letter of every word, D... T... O... P... Damn! Nothing!

Another dead end! How about the El Paso shooter? Did he leave any clues as to who could have inspired him?

**Panel 8:**
Well, there's this photo of guns that he posted. Maybe we can find some pattern in the way they are arranged!

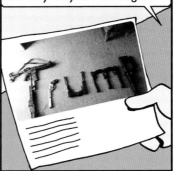

**Panel 9:**
Nah, they appear to be randomly strewn across the floor!

What is it?? What is the inspiration for this violence?!

NEXT WEEK: The search continues for the one factor that TRUMPS all the others!

8/19/19

# TOM the DANCING BUG

by RUBEN BOLLING

"I HEAR WHAT YOU'RE SAYING. SURE, YOU'RE SICK OF HEARING ABOUT TRUMP AND THAT HURRICANE THING. I KNOW, IT'S TIRESOME."

"BUT HIS ABSOLUTELY BIZARRE REACTION TO THE CRITICISM IS GENUINELY ALARMING."

"WE CAN'T SHRUG OFF HIS PATHOLOGIES AND ATTACKS ON DECENCY AND DEMOCRACY JUST BECAUSE IT'S EXHAUSTING TO KEEP CALLING THEM OUT."

"CAN WE LET OURSELVES BECOME IMMUNE TO HIS SEXISM AND RACISM? HIS SEXUAL ASSAULTS AND COZYING UP TO WHITE NATIONALISM?"

"I UNDERSTAND YOU'RE TIRED OF ALL THIS. BUT IF THE MEDIA STOPS COVERING TRUMP'S DERANGED BEHAVIOR BECAUSE IT OCCURS WITH 'TIRESOME' FREQUENCY..."

"...THEN IT'S COMPLICIT IN NORMALIZING THAT BEHAVIOR FOR THE VERY REASON IT'S SO URGENTLY THREATENING.

OH, I GUESS YOU'RE RIGHT. IT'S JUST, UGH! **ENOUGH** ABOUT TRUMP!

DIST. BY ANDREWS McMEEL SYNDICATION ~ ©2019 R. BOLLING ~ 1454 ~ TO JOIN THE INNER HIVE, GO TO tomthedancingbug.com

9/9/19

# TOM the DANCING BUG

## A MALTHUSIAN EXPERIMENT

by RUBEN BOLLING

It's based on a theory that goes back to the 19th century.

Put mice in an enclosed environment with abundant resources.

With no checks on their survival, they begin reproducing rapidly, creating a population explosion.

When the population reaches a breaking point, something interesting happens.

THERE ARE TOO MANY OF US, AND OUR ACTIVITY IS CHANGING OUR ENVIRONMENT!

WHAT ARE YOU TALKING ABOUT? THERE'S NOTHING WRONG, EVERYTHING IS FINE!

THAT PILE OF POOP IS GROWING!

YOU'RE IMAGINING THAT! I THINK IT'S GETTING SMALLER!

BUT OUR CALCULATIONS... HEY, YOU'RE PEEING ON OUR DATA!

I CALL IT RELAXING ENVIRONMENTAL REGULATIONS.

MY FOOD PELLET DISTRIBUTION COMPANY IS DOING GREAT! I'M NOT GOING TO JEOPARDIZE THAT BY PAYING FOR SOME FANCY CLEAN-UP SYSTEM.

BUT IF WE WORK TOGETHER TO...

YOU STINKING SOCIALIST! I'M A FREE-MARKET POOPER!

IT'S (COUGH) ALMOST TOO LATE! THINK OF THE CHILDREN!

NO! I'M... A (COUGH)...

...SKEPTIC.

Same result as always. The entire colony died.

Let's run the experiment again, but this time we don't give them Twitter...

9/16/19

DIST. BY ANDREWS McMEEL SYNDICATION — ©2019 R. BOLLING — 1456 — TO JOIN THE INNER HIVE, GO TO tomthedancingbug.com

9/23/19

# DONALD and JOHN
## a boy President and his Imaginary Publicist

9/30/19

# TOM the DANCING BUG

by RUBEN BOLLING

DIST. BY ANDREWS McMEEL SYNDICATION – ©2019 R. BOLLING – 1458 – TO JOIN THE INNER HIVE, GO TO tomthedancingbug.com

## THE Donald TRUMP MYSTERIES

I've got to investigate corruption!

I got a hot tip that a very top White House official's SON once got money from a foreign government!

I will throw the entire weight of the U.S.'s foreign policy and military aid programs behind investigating this!

Ukraine, the American people's money will be withheld from you until you fully investigate!

China on line 2!

Good Lord! A breakthrough! It wasn't just ONE son grabbing money, it was TWO!

And they were working not only for themselves, but for the company of their father -- THE TOP WHITE HOUSE OFFICIAL HIMSELF!

A warning, sir. The answer to this could affect the 2020 election...

I CARE NOT! I only care about corruption!

And his daughter and son-in-law got top positions but had absolutely no experience... OH, THE CORRUPTION!

And they continued to make hundreds of millions of dollars off connections in foreign governments! DISGRACEFUL!

HEA

I'm finding more! Foreign governments were throwing money at the father's hotels!

WAIT! Here's a secret document showing that the official tried to trade military aid for dirt on a political opponent!

CONTINUED NEXT WEEK –

It gets worse! The official and his family then set up a prison protection racket! Oh, where will the corruption end?!

10/7/19

DIST. BY ANDREWS McMEEL SYNDICATION — ©2019 R. BOLLING — 1459 — TO JOIN THE INNER HIVE, GO TO tomthedancingbug.com

LUCKY DUCKY
THE POOR LITTLE DUCK WHO'S RICH IN LUCK!

I... I'VE **DONE** IT! MY LIFELONG DREAM FINALLY **REALIZED!**

HA! THERE YOU ARE, **LUCKY DUCKY!** PICKING UP YOUR MEASLY PAYCHECK!

FOR THE **FIRST TIME**, WE BILLIONAIRES NOW PAY A **LOWER TAX RATE** THAN YOU POOR PEOPLE!

YOU'RE POOR, SO YOU ALWAYS FOUND SOME WAY TO WIN, BUT I MADE SURE **I'D** WIN THIS TIME!

YES, I HAD TO MAKE SOME... QUESTIONABLE ALLIANCES.

MY NEW ASSOCIATES ARE... UM...

HOLLINGSWORTH! COME HAVE THE VODKA!

WELL, THEY'RE...

YOU HAVE THE THING FOR VLAD?

COMPROMISES WERE MADE...

NOW IS TIME TO PARTY!

YOUR COUNTRY IS VERY FUN TO HAVE!

UH...

GIDDYAP!

WHAT'S WRONG, H.? YOU LOOK AS SAD AS A KID IN A CAGE! **BWAHAHAHA!**

ER...I'VE GOT TO GO...

SURE YOU DON'T WANT ONE OF THE GIRLS?

THEY ARE VERY YOUNG...

COME BACK SOON. OR ELSE.

LUCKY DUCKY!

GOTCHA?

10/14/19

TOM the DANCING BUG by RUBEN BOLLING

DIST. BY ANDREWS McMEEL SYNDICATION – ©2019 R. BOLLING – 1460 – TO JOIN THE INNER HIVE, GO TO tomthedancingbug.com

The Don

Nice aid package you got here, Zelensky. Shame if something stopped it from gettin' to you.

W-what do you want, Mr. Trump?

I'm just sayin'... You could dig up some dirt on a certain individual, let's call him Joe.

FREEZE! THIS IS A BUST!!

Whoa, don't get excited, copper.

HEY, I SAID FREEZE!

What! I have an appointment in Austria!

GET THOSE OTHER GUYS!

You were threatening this man!

I just made a suggestion. There was no quid pro quo.

You were here, Mick. Did he say there was a quid pro quo?

Of course he did! GET OVER IT!!

AHA! So you admit there was quid pro quo!

I never said that! Stop twisting my words!

Yeah, Recep. Go ahead in.

We finally nailed you, Don!

My goodness! Look, officer! An ethnic cleansing in progress!

AAHH!

HELP!

You... you monster! That's not going to work!

Can't blame a guy for tryin'.

You don't seem worried at all.

Ah, that's because I know a guy.

A guy?

Yeah, I already know the jury foreman for my trial.

NOT GUIL.

Not yet, Mitch.

10/21/19

**TOM the DANCING BUG**

by RUBEN BOLLING

AMERICA. 2019.

THE PRESIDENT'S LAWYERS ARGUE IN COURT THAT A UNITED STATES PRESIDENT CANNOT BE INDICTED *OR INVESTIGATED* FOR ANY CRIME. *INCLUDING MURDER.*

WHEN THIS PRINCIPLE IS ADOPTED BY THE COURT, IT IS THE DAWN OF... PRESIDENTIAL PURGE.

SURVIVE THE ADMINISTRATION.

10/28/19

# SUPER-FUN-PAK COMIX

DIST. BY ANDREWS McMEEL SYNDICATION - © 2019 R. Bolling -1462- TO JOIN THE INNER HIVE, GO TO tomthedancingbug.com

## ZONE OF SURPRISING, IRONIC PLOT TWISTS

I HOPE THE PLASTIC SURGERY WORKED! — SHE WAS SO HIDEOUS!

GASP! — NO! IT FAILED!

SHE'S STILL DRAWN TOO CARTOONY!

## PERCIVAL DUNWOODY, IDIOT TIME-TRAVELER FROM 1909

HAPPY BIRTHDAY, PERCIVAL! — I HOPE IT ISN'T A YELLOW AND GREEN TIE!

ER...HEY!

THIS ISN'T YOUR FIRST TIME IN THIS MOMENT, IS IT?

I CAN KEEP DOING THIS UNTIL YOU GET IT RIGHT.

## FOR NO APPARENT REASON: DARTHFIELD

THIS IS THE BEST LASAGNA IN THE PARSEC.

ACTUALLY, PARSEC IS A UNIT OF DISTANCE.

ENJOY A FEW PARSECS OF THE FORCE.

URK

## FOOTPRINTS IN THE SAND

In my most troubled times, why is there only one set of footprints?

Why, that was when I carried you.

Then why does one set go up to that seaside bar?

Let us not dwell on footprints, my son.

## CREATURE FROM THE BLACK LAGOON

AUGH! IT'S THE CREATURE FROM THE BLACK LAGOON!

ACTUALLY, I'M THE CREATURE FROM THE BLACK LAGOON'S MONSTER!

THIS IS THE CREATURE FROM THE BLACK LAGOON! HI.

## THE NEW YORKER CINEMATIC UNIVERSE

"This threat is too great! All allies must be gathered!"

"I came as quickly as I could! What is the problem, Middle-Aged-Couple-In-Armchairs-Man?"

"Now that Desert-Island-Man is here, we must... Oh, no! It's too late!!"

"That's right! Feel the wrath of Boss-Behind-A-Desk-Man! I will destroy all in my path!"

NEXT: MILDLY HUMOROUS CAPITALISM RUN AMOK!

11/4/19

TOM the
DANCING BUG

by
Ruben
Bolling

YOUR BIBLE JUST GOT TRUMPED!

Introducing the
**THIRD**
NEWER, BEST

# Testament

The teachings and story of **DONALD J. TRUMP,**
billionaire and pussy-grabber

### Shun the Stranger

"You are disgusting and subhuman."

### Sermon on the Hotel Grounds

"Blessed are the Me."

### Repress the Children

"Lock 'em up."

### Render unto Caesar

"...but cheat the Hell out of Uncle Sam."

## Behold the Miracles of the Donald

Avoiding venereal diseases despite indiscriminate sexual intercourse

Transforming a written admission of stealing from his own charity into a dove

Diverting the course of mighty hurricanes

Healing of his own bone spurs

And yet for all His Holiness, he is persecuted simply for committing secular crimes that benefit His own Holy Self.

**Own this Essential Addition to Your Bible!**

*Only* **$59.99!**

Available only in Twitter-Video form OR Two-Page-Summary form!

11/11/19

# DONALD and JOHN
## a boy PrEsidEnt and his Imaginary Publicist

DIST. BY ANDREWS McMEEL SYNDICATION – ©2019 R. BOLLING – 1464 – TO JOIN THE INNER HIVE, GO TO tomthedancingbug.com

SO, ALL I DID WAS TRY TO HIJACK PUBLIC FUNDS AND U.S. FOREIGN POLICY...

...TO EXTORT A COUNTRY INTO SUPPORTING MY SMEAR ATTACK ON MY POLITICAL RIVAL!

NOW I'M IN TROUBLE!

A WORLD OF TROUBLE!

THAT'S IT!! I'LL GO LIVE ON ANOTHER WORLD!

YOU CAN'T STAY ON THE GOLF COURSE FOREVER...

I MADE THIS PORTAL TO A WORLD WHERE I'M NOT A BAD BOY!

FOXIFIER FOX

THERE! IN THIS WORLD, WHATEVER I SAY IS TRUE!

LET'S TRY IT. ⇒AHEM⇐ I'M AN INTREPID, DEDICATED CORRUPTION FIGHTER!

WOW! I GOT MY OWN CHYRON TOO!

FOX LITTLE DONALD: HERO

GOSH, IN THIS WORLD, I'M A HERO TO ALL!

LITTLE DONALD IS NOT WEAK!

LITTLE DONALD IS SUPE

We LOVE DONALD ♥

I MAKE PERFECT PHONE CALLS, AND EVERYONE KNOWS IT!

AND ANYONE WHO REVEALS INCRIMINATING INFO AGAINST ME IS A BIASED MONSTER!

WHAT ABOUT THE GUY WHO RELEASED THE PHONE CALL "TRANSCRIPT"?

THAT WAS ME, SO I'LL MAKE AN EXCEPTION.

PROBLEM SOLVED! I'LL JUST STAY IN THIS WORLD, WHERE I'M A SELFLESS DO-GOODER, FOREVER!

HOW COME YOU LEFT THAT WORLD?

FOXIF FOX

I CAN'T DO MY CRIMES THERE!

WELL, I'M SURE YOU'LL VISIT OFTEN.

FOXIF FOX

11/18/19

TOM the DANCING BUG

by RUBEN BOLLING

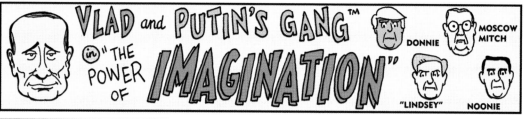
VLAD and PUTIN'S GANG™ in "THE POWER OF IMAGINATION"
DONNIE · MOSCOW MITCH · "LINDSEY" · NOONIE

GOSH, GANG! EVERYONE KNOWS THE **RUSSIANS** HACKED THE DEMOCRATIC NATIONAL COMMITTEE TO HELP **US**!
WE'RE IN TROUBLE!

NOT NECESSARILY, GANG!
VLADIMIR PUTIN!

YOU CAN ALWAYS USE... **POWER OF IMAGINATION** TO GET OUT OF ANY JAM!

MAYBE I HACKED DNC... BUT IN OUR IMAGINATION, MAYBE *UKRAINE* DID IT!
HUH?

WE CAN IMAGINE: UKRAINE **FRAMED** RUSSIANS AND THEN LEAKED DNC EMAILS TO HELP **HILLARY**!

BUT THAT DON'T MAKE EVEN A LICK OF SENSE!
BUT IT'S **BEAUTIFUL**! THAT'S ALL THAT MATTERS ...IN YOUR *IMAGINATION*!

HEY, IF YOU TRY REALLY HARD, YOU CAN ALMOST BELIEVE IT!
I BELIEVE IT, AND I'M NOT TRYING HARD.

VLAD'S STORY IS INFECTIOUSLY WHIMSICAL!
WE'LL PRETEND IT'S **TRUE**!
WE'LL DO IT!

YOU'D BETTER, BECAUSE PEE TAPE IS VERY, VERY REAL!
IT'S THE POWER OF **IMAGINATION**!
the End

11/25/19

# TOM the DANCING BUG

by RUBEN BOLLING

DIST. BY ANDREWS McMEEL SYNDICATION – ©2019 R.BOLLING – 1466 – TO JOIN THE INNER HIVE, GO TO tomthedancingbug.com

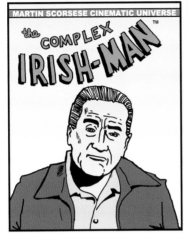

**MARTIN SCORSESE CINEMATIC UNIVERSE**

the COMPLEX IRISH-MAN™

IRISH-MAN IS IN HIS IRISH-HIDEOUT WHEN...

THIS CANNOT STAND!! I'VE GOT TO TRANSFORM AND GATHER THE GROUP!

ACTIVATE DE-AGING POWER TO 30 YEARS OLD!

BUT STILL LOOK VAGUELY LIKE I'M 76.

GOOD-FELLA!™ RAGING BULL!™ YOU MADE IT!

THIS BETTER BE GOOD! I GAINED 45 POUNDS FOR THIS!

AS YOU KNOW, WE ARE CHARACTERS WHO STRUGGLE WITH VIOLENCE, IMMORALITY, GUILT, AND THE CATHOLIC RELIGION IN THE CONTEXT OF MID-CENTURY AMERICAN ORGANIZED CRIME.

BUT THESE *NEW GUYS* ARE MUSCLING IN ON OUR TERRITORY! THEY TELL THE *SAME STORY OVER AND OVER!*

WE GOTTA DO SOMETHING!

IT'S GO TIME!! ATTACK...

... WITH A WELL-REASONED, THOUGHTFUL OP-ED EXPLAINING THAT THERE SHOULD BE ROOM FOR DIFFERENT STYLES OF MOVIES...

SPLAT

DID YOU HEAR SOMETHING?

SOUNDED LIKE PSYCHOLOGICALLY COMPLEX CHARACTERS GETTING SQUASHED!

CINEMA MULT

**NEXT WEEK:** *OSCAR REVENGE!!*

12/2/19

TOM the DANCING BUG

by RUBEN BOLLING

The Donald J. Trump
Historical Players
PRESENT

**THE DRAFTING
OF THE
UNITED STATES
CONSTITUTION**

Upper East Side, 1492 or when-ever. Three big, tough Founding Fathers out of central casting discuss the Constitution.

What's the best way to do Democracy?

The Electoral College! It'll be the main part of the Constitution, and it's the best way to express the will of the people!

Done!

Here are your Diet Cokes and cans of aerosol hair spray!

Thanks, Betsy Ross. We're going to celebrate!

Now go type up our notes!

She's a 6 at best, but we keep her around because she can sew and type and she's got a rack!

Okay, I'm done typing up the Constitution on my olden-timey computer. I'll go to sleep now.

That night...

IMPEACHMENT FOR BRIBERY OR OTHER HIGH

KLIK
KLIK - KLIK KLIK
KLIK

I just printed out the Constitution.

Hmm... Good, it's got the Electoral College and all the best words.

Wait a minute!! What's this part about IMPEACHMENT?? That nonsense word doesn't belong in a Constitution!

It's some kind of long typo!

Betsy Ross! This could subvert the sacred Electoral College! Remove it immediately!

No, wait. Why bother? Future generations will know that it's utterly meaningless...

... and could never apply to a guy with a very large brain who withholds security assistance to a foreign country and then politely asks it to investigate a really corrupt, bad Democrat!

That would be **perfect!**

God Bless America

DIST. BY ANDREWS McMEEL SYNDICATION — ©2019 R. BOLLING — 1467 — TO JOIN THE INNER HIVE, GO TO tomthedancingbug.com

12/9/19

# TOM the DANCING BUG

by RUBEN BOLLING

## DoNald and JOHN
### a boy PrEsident and his Imaginary Publicist

DIST. BY ANDREWS McMEEL SYNDICATION — ©2019 R. BOLLING — 1468 — TO JOIN THE INNER HIVE, GO TO tomthedancingbug.com

12/16/19

This comic appeared in the Family Issue of *The Nib Magazine*, published January, 2019.

# Donald and John

## by Ruben Bolling

# a boy Presidential candidate and his Imaginary Publicist

In early October 2016, with the election bearing down, Bolling launched a separate, limited-time, almost daily comic strip based on his Donald and John comics. It was published on TheNib.com, concluding the day after the election. The series won the National Cartoonists Society Best Online Cartoon Award in 2017.

# DoNald and JoHN
## a boy PrEsidential caNdidate and his Imaginary Publicist

10/7/16

10/8/16

10/10/16

10/10/16

# DONaLd and JOHN
## a boy PrEsidential caNdidate and his ImaginarY Publicist

10/12/16

10/13/16

10/14/16

10/17/16

# DoNald and JOHN
## a boy PrEsidential caNdidate and his Imaginary Publicist

10/18/16

10/19/16

10/20/16

10/21/16

# DoNald and JoHN
## a boy PrEsidential caNdidate and his Imaginary Publicist

10/24/16

10/25/16

10/26/16

10/27/16

# DoNald and JOHN
## a boy PrEsidential candidate and his Imaginary Publicist

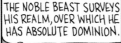

THE NOBLE BEAST SURVEYS HIS REALM, OVER WHICH HE HAS ABSOLUTE DOMINION.

BUT THERE IS CHANGE IN THE AIR. COULD THE REIGN OF HIM AND HIS KIND BE ENDING?

IT CANNOT BE! IT IS FOREVER HIS BIRTHRIGHT TO ACT ON HIS EVERY WHIM!

DONALD, YOU HAVE TO **ASK** BEFORE YOU GRAB!

OH, MAN!

10/28/16

HIS SVELTE, PERFECT FORM TRAVERSES THE LANDSCAPE, A FEARED KILLING MACHINE.

HIS IS AN IDEAL BODY, AND NO PARTS OF IT ARE COMICALLY, HUMILIATINGLY TINY.

WHEN HE EMITS HIS MIGHTY ROAR, IT IS NOT AT ALL IN COMPENSATION FOR SUCH TINY BODY PARTS!

ROAR

ANYONE EVER TELL YOU YOUR HANDS ARE TINY?

**THEY ARE NOT!**

10/31/16

THE MURDER RATE IN THE U.S. IS THE HIGHEST IT'S BEEN IN 45 YEARS.

UM, ACTUALLY, THAT'S TOTALLY FALSE.

SO YOU THINK I SHOULD... ABSOLUTELY...

**THE MURDER RATE IN THE U.S. IS THE HIGHEST IT'S BEEN IN 45 YEARS!!**

...SAY IT LOUDER.

11/1/16

DONALD THE SPY IS IN MOSCOW -- WHAT WILL THE RUSSIAN AGENTS DO TO TRY TO TURN HIM AGAINST AMERICA?

HYPNOSIS? BLACKMAIL? THREATS? *IT WON'T WORK!* NOTHING CAN SWAY DONALD THE SPY'S LOYALTY TO THE U.S.A.!

DONALD, WE'D LIKE TO INVEST IN YOUR BUSINESS. MILLIONS OF RUBLES!

NATO IS OBSOLETE! RUSSIA NEVER INVADED UKRAINE! PUTIN IS GREAT!

11/2/16

# DoNald and JOHN
## a boy PrEsidential caNdidate and his Imaginary Publicist

11/3/16

11/4/16

11/7/16

11/8/16

# DONALD and JOHN

## a boy PrEsidential candidate and his Imaginary Publicist

11/9/16